FlashPoint

For Young Adults

Ignite Your Potential!

By Kenneth W. Olan

Houston, Texas
2006

Lynn Scott Publishing
4415 Magnolia Lane, #101
Sugar Land, Texas 77478

ISBN# 0-9773155-0-9

www.EveryAdvantage.net

Book Production Team
Publishing Consulting & Interior Design — Rita Mills of The Book Connection
Editing — Peggy Stautberg and Judy King

Cover Design—Gateway Design, Inc.— Houston, Texas

The paper used in this publication meets the requirements of the American National Standard for Permanence of Paper for Printed Library Materials Z39.48-1984.

Printed in the United States of America

To my wife Susan for your unwavering love and
support. You are my foundation.

To my children Rachael and Michael for keeping me
connected to what is really important.
You are the future.

To my mother Estelle for your strength of character
and incredible resilience. You amaze me.

To my late father Sol for his humanity, his love of
learning and for inspiring me to share what I
know to help others. He made a difference.

And to my entire extended family . . .
just for being you.

What's Inside

Acknowledgments

There are many people who have either touched or supported this important project.

First and foremost, the *FlashPoint* series would not have gotten this far without the help of my dear friends Connie Haywood of Gateway Design for your steadfast encouragement, wonderful insight, and generous access to your talented team and creative resources, and Nancy Lerner, for your consistent inspiration, unwavering confidence, and critical entrée to the Teen Chat Group from whom I've received so much valuable input and feedback. My gratitude is without bounds.

Thanks also to Beth Carls and Amy Looper of MindOH! for your daily dose of entrepreneurial energy, ideas and enthusiasm. I also extend my sincerest appreciation to Bob and Rita Zeleny, Laurie Bricker, Buddy Cox, Jim Evans, Dina Kohleffel, Michele Pola, Lavaille Lavette, Jordan Shenker, Michael Garfield, Ryan Dolibois, Mary Nesbitt, Karol Musher, Barry Levine, Steve Maislin, Sara Selber, Barbara Vilutis, Dave Martin, Lindsay Smolenski, and Sarah Glover for your input to, and ongoing interest in, this project.

I extend special thanks to my book manager, Rita Mills, for your guidance and patience.

Finally, I'd like to thank authors Robert Allen, Les Brown, Tony Robbins, Jim Rohn, Dr. Denis Waitley, and the late Earl Nightingale, each of whose works have had a particularly profound impact on my own self-understanding and the development of this book.

One last note. This book is the culmination of over 20 years of observations, research, opinions and my own view on the subject of personal achievement. Trying to figure out with 100% certainty exactly who should be credited for what is impossible. So if any of the thoughts that have influenced me have inadvertently become my own, or if I have given improper credit, I promise to acknowledge fully any sources who bring their contributions to my attention.

The Genius of an Apple Seed

I once heard something that got me thinking about how we can live our lives. A question was asked: "When an apple seed is planted, how quickly will it start to grow?" The simple answer is, "The seed will start growing as soon as it can." It will sprout exactly when it can gather enough water and have the right soil temperature to do so. Common sense, right?

The next question to consider might be, "Once the apple seed begins to grow, how quickly and how big will the apple tree grow?" The answer, of course, is "The apple tree will grow as quickly and as big as it can grow." The tree doesn't say, "Hey, I think I'll wait a while before I start to grow." It doesn't think, "Maybe I'll just grow a little bit and stop." It doesn't consider, "Maybe I can grow on my own. I don't need any stupid water or sun or nutrients." Instead the tree just takes in of all the resources it can to grow as big as it can and as fast as it can.

Now obviously trees don't think . . . at least as far as we know. But every tree is "programmed" with the potential to grow regardless of the particular environment it is in. Every tree will stretch its branches out as far as it can to take in all the sun it can, and it will grow its roots so that it can get all of the water and nutrients possible from the soil. A tree always "wants" to make the most of its potential as early as possible, and it does all it can to do just that.

So how about you? Are you smarter than an apple seed? Are you going to do all you can to have a successful life?

In some ways the tree is lucky. It can't "think" about all the reasons why it can't grow, so it just grows all it can. Human beings, on the other hand, don't always make the most of their potential. Sometimes they don't know how. Sometimes they think they're doing the most they can but really aren't, and sometimes for one reason or another they simply don't try to live life to the fullest.

I hope that you're reading *FlashPoint* because you have an interest in learning how to make the most of your potential as soon as you can, and by as much as you can. I mean, why not? That's what life is all about, isn't it?

Getting the Most from *FlashPoint*

> **"*FlashPoint* is designed to help you get ahead on getting ahead in life."**

The purpose of this book is *not* to tell you how to live your life. Nobody should be able to do that. How you live is up to you. Instead I wrote this book and its "sister" book, *FlashPoint II: Accelerate Your Success!*, to show you some powerful ways to help you more quickly create the satisfying and fulfilling life you want to live. To put it simply *FlashPoint* is designed to help you "get ahead on getting ahead in life."

In addition to what you'll be reading in the following pages, this book is complemented by a number of unique and valuable personal development tools that you'll find in the *Making Connections: Plug-It-In and Work-It-Out Tool Kit* in the back of the book. You can also find the same tools in a larger, full-page, printable format at www.EveryAdvantage.net.

If you decide to use the website, and I hope you do, you may want to take a moment right now to look at www.EveryAdvantage.net. That way you'll be familiar with the website when you are ready to start using it.

Okay, time to move ahead!

Future Thinking

Imagine yourself 5 or 10 years from now. What do you think your life will look like? Will you be happy? Will you have the type of friends you want?

What kind of physical shape will you be in? Will you have gotten the education you wanted? Will you be comfortable financially, or maybe even be rich?

Whatever you imagine your life will be, I'm sure you'll want to see yourself as "successful" at some point based on whatever that word means to you.

Now take a moment and think again about the successful "you" of 5 to 10 years from now. How do you imagine you'll be feeling? What do you think you will have needed to do in order to accomplish your achievements and to get to that feeling of success? In other words how did you have to *feel* and *think* in order to get there? What do you suppose you'd have to know? What actions would you have had to take?

Interesting questions, don't you think? I certainly don't expect you to have the answers to them . . . yet. But how much better do you suppose your life could be if you learned how to maximize your success *now* while you're younger? What if you understood how to think, and what to do, in order to accomplish greater things sooner? What *more* could you accomplish if you didn't have to wait 10, 20, or more years until you started to figure it all out? How much more could you achieve?

Remember the tree? How much bigger would it be today if it were planted 10 years earlier?

Figuring out exactly how things work in this world can take a lifetime, quite literally. The good news is that it doesn't have to take decades to piece together many of life's secrets or wisdom. Like any other natural resource, the knowledge is there, waiting to be discovered, uncovered, and used. You just have to know where to look and what tools to use to uncover that knowledge.

Well, you've come to a great place to help you start to figure it all out. This book and personal achievement system will be helpful to you if you want to get better results out of life. The principles you'll learn apply to *everyone*, whether he or she is 14 years old, 16 years old, 26, or 86.

What you'll learn here will not "make you" change anything you don't want to change. You'll simply become better equipped to accomplish what you want to accomplish sooner and with greater ease.

I wrote this book because after years of studying what makes "successful" people successful, I realized something. It occurred to me that if I'd known, or had at least been aware of, the things you'll be learning here when I was younger, my journey in life could have been so much more fun, focused, productive, and less of a mystery.

Over the years I've seen a lot of personal development information in the marketplace aimed at "seasoned" adults. Why do you suppose that is? Could it be because many adults didn't get things "figured out" better earlier in life? Really, think about it. If the adults whom those books are written for had discovered more of life's insights earlier, they'd have less need to seek them out later.

The bottom line is that if you learn and use just a fraction of what you'll be offered here, you can make dramatic leaps in your quest for personal achievement. Likewise if you use a lot of what you'll learn here, more "power" to you . . . literally.

All That

Before we go any further, I thought it would be helpful for you to understand exactly where I'm coming from as you read this book, so allow me to take a moment or two to explain.

When I was a young adult, I had the world right where I wanted it . . . or at least *thought* that I did. I saw myself as smart, ambitious, creative, and a bunch of other cool adjectives. My family wasn't wealthy . . . actually quite the contrary. However I was well liked in school, entrepreneurial, and always had a few bucks in my pocket.

If I didn't know better (and it turns out I didn't), I would have said that it seemed that things were going "just as I had planned."

But things didn't stay seemingly stress-free forever. As time passed and as I progressed on through my college years, "life" became increasingly more complicated. School, jobs, dating, family commitments, workouts, and so on were all competing for the limited time (and brain space) I had available.

Then one day it struck me like a ton of bricks. I realized that life wasn't going to be exactly the way I wanted it or planned it. Why, you ask. Because I wasn't really clear about what I wanted, so how could I have *possibly* planned anything? So I wondered, how could that have happened? Then it struck me.

You see, formal schooling had taught me a lot about academic subjects like math and history, but it fell short in teaching me about life. Perhaps that sounds familiar to you. School didn't really help me determine what to do with my life or how to plan for my future, at least not directly.

You see, the schools had the authority to teach only the subjects on the state's "approved curriculum" list, and things haven't changed much in that respect today. So in looking back, I now recognize that there was a critical gap in my education. School certainly helped me become "book smart," but it didn't do much to help me learn how to be "life smart."

You might wonder, "Which is more important, school smarts (academics) or life smarts?" The answer is they're both important in different ways.

Academic knowledge is needed to help you bring your life smarts into focus. What you learn in school enables you to make "real life" distinctions and decisions more quickly. In school you learn how to compare, measure, contrast, and otherwise understand the world around you.

Hey, I realize that I use only a portion of what I learned in school on any given day, but that's not really the point. The most important thing I learned in school was *how* to learn. How to use my brain to think. That's really the key.

We do learn a lot of what we ultimately know in life through experience. In turn experience helps us recognize patterns. In the same way math, science, history, and so on help us learn how to see patterns and how to recognize things for what they are. It's not the academic information we learn in school, in and of itself, that's the key. Certainly it's important. But it's the *process* of learning how to learn that adds so much value to *who* and *what* we become. It's called critical thinking skills. That's what we get from school smarts, and critical thinking skills are just that . . . *critical*.

Life smarts, on the other hand, work with what you learn in school to help you grow personally and professionally, so the two together form a powerful combination.

Here's another way to look at it. Academic achievement, including high school, college, or higher education, is the ticket that gets you into the "big game" of life. Getting into the game is important. However it's your life smarts that will determine whether you're ultimately an "all-star" or on the "second string" team.

> **❝ I realized that life wasn't going to be exactly the way I wanted it or planned it. Why? Because I wasn't really clear about what I wanted, so how could I have possibly planned anything?❞**

Oh, *Now* I Get it!

When I was younger, I didn't have a clear understanding of just how much I *didn't* know. Instead I thought I knew an awful lot. I was sure that once I got loose in the real world, I was going to kick some proverbial "butt."

It wasn't until much later that I figured out it would be *my butt* that was going to be kicked around a bit . . . or a lot . . . along the way.

To my disappointment by my early twenties I hadn't earned the money I'd wanted to, and I wasn't particularly happy with my life. I was in a job that I didn't like, out of shape, and my love life was mediocre at best.

Although I did pretty well in my first job, I noticed I was competing with a lot of other people, some of whom were also quite talented, for the management job I *thought* I wanted.

"Wait a second," I thought. "You mean my skills and personality alone are not enough to take me to the top? Other people will be competing with me? Who came up with that lousy, bogus concept?"

With my newly found awareness I began to take a closer look at my life and myself. I wanted to know what was going wrong and if there was someone else I could *blame* for this obvious mistake of fate. Or could it be that my lack of progress in several areas of my life was due to something I did or didn't do? I wondered if maybe it had something to do with the way I thought about things. I was determined to find out exactly what was happening.

With a burning desire to find answers I started researching the subjects of success, happiness, and personal achievement. In the process I learned so much of value that I eventually made a hobby out of exploring and applying the concepts I was learning about the intriguing subject of personal "success."

During my years of research I slowly began to piece together the common characteristics of successful people. I learned what they did, how they did it, and how they thought. To be clear, by "successful" I don't necessarily mean financially successful. We'll define exactly what success means to *you* a little later.

Over the next decade and following about five thousand hours of research, I noticed something. I kept hearing the same messages, themes, and patterns from virtually all the experts in the field of personal achievement. The same principles of success appeared to apply to everyone.

As I learned the common characteristics that successful people shared, I began to experience a number of what I call "light bulb" experiences. You know, the way you feel when you've heard something anywhere from once to fifty million times and you finally say to yourself, "Ohhh, *now* I get it!" A realization, so to speak. An awakening of awareness.

It's kind of like looking in the kitchen cabinet for the saltshaker, and you can't seem to find it. Then all of a sudden you notice it's the closest thing to your nose, staring you right in the face. The saltshaker was there the whole time. You just didn't see it. You didn't see it because, at some level, you didn't focus on what you were looking for, and in some cases you didn't even *know* what you were looking for.

Life is full of such experiences. There are lots of things you don't "get" until you *do* get them. It's part of the natural learning process. There is always information out there to be found. You just have to know where, and how, to look for it.

One especially bright "flash of light" occurred in my head not too long ago that led me to write this book. In a moment of deep thought I realized that I could have learned a lot of the "secrets" to personal achievement and success much earlier in life if only I had someone to teach them to me. Someone to explain things to me in a way I could understand considering my age and experience. Someone to whom I would be willing to listen and who would make sure I "got" it.

I realize that my parents tried to share some important wisdom with me, and although I may have grabbed onto a little bit of it here or there, I had my own way of thinking about things. I had my own "belief" system. I'm sure you can relate. (We'll learn more about how your personal beliefs affect your life later on.)

So anyway I decided to take what I'd realized . . . that one can actually become wiser sooner . . . a step further. I thought, what if I could teach others many of the things I wish I'd known when I was younger? Things like:

> **66 Wait a second,"** I thought. "You mean my skills and personality alone are not enough to take me to the top? Other people will be competing with me? Who came up with that lousy, bogus concept?**99**

- ◆ How to understand your personal purpose and passion.
- ◆ How others' definition of success doesn't have to be yours.
- ◆ The impact of perseverance on one's success.
- ◆ How to communicate more effectively.
- ◆ How to manage your thoughts to give you more power.
- ◆ How to deal with others who try to influence you.
- ◆ How to take good risks and make better decisions.
- ◆ How to market yourself.
- ◆ How to handle money, and so on.

After doing a lot of research with high-school-aged students, I knew that helping people get what they want out of life faster could be done. I saw clearly that success and self-understanding can be sped up. That's when I decided to create *FlashPoint* and write this book and then a second book: *FlashPoint: Harness Your Power!*

My hope is that by reading *FlashPoint* and using what you learn here, you'll figure out your own life-success formula much faster. Doing so will help you speed up your rate of personal achievement, and you'll be more likely to have an increased sense of fulfillment and personal happiness.

Knowing What's Down the Road

To explain how you'll use what you learn in this book, let's start out with an analogy. By the way you'll find that I use a lot of analogies, because comparing new ideas to things you already know will help you understand them that much faster.

Let's say you're going across town to your friend's house and when you get there he or she asks you if you saw any blue minivans on your way over. You'd most likely look at him or her in a puzzled way and say, "I don't know. *Why* would I pay attention to something like that?"

But what would have happened if your friend had called you before you left your house and said, "The radio station is having a contest. On your way over here be sure to keep an eye out for blue minivans. One of them has a purple pinstripe going down the side and a license plate that says 'FM 101.5.' If you spot it, write down where you see it. We can call it in to the station and win front row seats and backstage passes to Saturday's big concert." Would you pay any more attention to blue minivans then?

In that situation you'd have an advantage by knowing, in advance, exactly what to look for to win the prize. In the same way you'll be more ready to see and reap the rewards you want in life if you know early on in life's journey what important "life clues" to look for. It's kind of like knowing the questions on a test in advance.

Well, *life is a test* that involves a series of choices, and I hope to help you get to some of the answers earlier. At the very least I'll give you some ideas about what to study, what to learn, and what you may want to pay attention to in order to get the results you want. I want to make you aware of some important stuff now. That way you'll be able to recognize and take advantage of more opportunities that come your way throughout your life (like the blue minivan).

In order to do that, you may find me repeating some things just to make sure you "get" them. Let me repeat that. You may notice that I repeat certain things to make sure you catch what I'm saying because I want to make sure you notice and remember them.

Okay, let's get started.

How You Learn

Learning is a science just like biology or math. If you know the "rules," it becomes easier to understand, to do, and to stick with. That's why we're covering this subject first. If you have a realistic understanding of how you can expect your learning to progress, you'll be more likely to stick with your personal development plan.

Let's start by doing a fun, short activity. You'll find this activity called "Number Hunt" on page 166 of your *Making Connections: Plug-It-In and Work-It-Out Tool Kit.* If you prefer, you can also find this activity on www.EveryAdvantage.net that you can print out and use.

Before you begin, make sure you have a watch or a clock nearby with a second hand on it, since the exercise requires you to time yourself.

This exercise should take you only about four minutes to complete. Have fun!

Look Familiar?

Okay, I'm going to assume you did the "Number Hunt" activity.

By doing that exercise, you experienced what happens when you become more familiar with something. In this case, after each try you became more familiar with the layout of the numbers on the page. If you were to do the same exercise enough times, eventually you'd be able to do it without even thinking about it. It would seem "natural." The same thing will happen when you use the success principles you'll learn here in *FlashPoint.*

This simple exercise points out a couple of important things to remember. First, you shouldn't expect to master anything the first time you try doing it, including what you'll learn in *FlashPoint.* Sometimes things take a bit of time to get good at, so be realistic.

The second thing to remember is the more you do something, the more familiar you become with it, and the more familiar you become with something, the easier you'll find it is to do. I know that's not rocket science, but it is something you need to keep in mind as we move forward.

In the same way it's important to understand that you will want to use the knowledge and skills you'll be learning here in order to master the information and use it to *your* advantage. Your familiarity with the concepts we'll cover will be the first key to feeling comfortable with them, but your ease and mastery will develop as you *apply* what you learn.

The Four Stages of Learning

Learning something new can be frustrating at times. However if you understand *why* it can be frustrating, learning can actually be easier.

According to psychologist Dr. Abraham Maslow, there are four distinct stages of learning virtually anything. Just like with the "Number Hunt" activity you just did, with each stage of learning, the things you learn become more and more "natural" to you until they feel natural or automatic.

As you use the things you'll learn in *FlashPoint,* you can expect to pass through all four stages of learning. You'll discover what you don't know, then you'll learn it, and then you'll become good at the skills you learn until you can use them with ease.

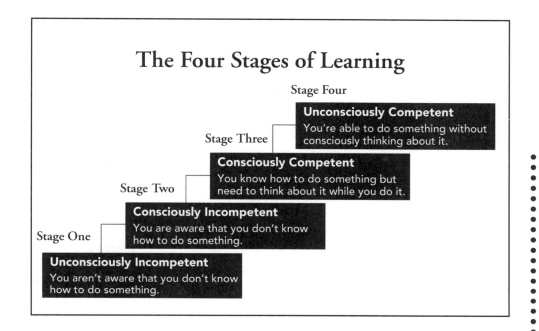

The Four Stages of Learning

Stage Four

Unconsciously Competent
You're able to do something without consciously thinking about it.

Stage Three

Consciously Competent
You know how to do something but need to think about it while you do it.

Stage Two

Consciously Incompetent
You are aware that you don't know how to do something.

Stage One

Unconsciously Incompetent
You aren't aware that you don't know how to do something.

Feeling Skeptical?

The first thing we need to do is break through whatever doubts you may might have about how, or whether, the information in this book applies to you. That's normal.

And since I want you to feel confident that what you'll be learning here is going to be helpful to you, I'll tell you up front how I've approached things:

◆ First I did my homework to know what is fact and what isn't. I've listed many of my resources in the back of the book.

◆ Second I try to avoid offering advice on anything I could be wrong about.

If you still have doubts about the value of what you'll be learning here, you'll just have to decide for yourself if you are willing to explore the possibilities.

To sum this up, I'd like to paraphrase a concept from the Greek philosopher Plato. He said, "Those who think that they're so smart that they don't need to learn anything new will eventually be followers of those who are dumber."

Think about it. — Okay, let's move on.

Knowing How to Be Successful

One big difference between successful and unsuccessful people is that successful people somehow "know" how to be successful. Successful people have learned how to achieve their success through reading, trial and error, or by learning from other successful people.

The fact is that very few people achieve high levels of success without help from anyone else. The most successful people have all received some sort of teaching or training in order for them to understand what to do and when to do it. The fact is we can learn only so much on our own. So let's get going together to help you achieve at the highest levels and discover ways to feel even better about yourself and your future.

Here's What to Expect

In the following pages we'll cover a wide range of important subjects related to personal achievement. You can find a list of what we'll cover at "What's Inside," the table of contents pages, in the front of the book.

By the time you've finished each chapter of *FlashPoint*, you should be prepared to take advantage of the information you've learned to help you speed up your rate of personal achievement.

Please keep in mind that the objective here is not to finish the book quickly. Instead you should learn at whatever pace is comfortable to you. If it takes you a month, or even 6 months, to get through, that's okay. Nothing worthwhile happens over night. It's better to understand and get good at something, and then move on to the next thing, than it is to move too quickly and be familiar with a lot of things but great at nothing. So again, work at a pace that works for you.

Walt Disney used to say, "Don't just give your audience what they want. Give them what you know they need and will help them." Well, you are my audience, and that is exactly what I hope to do.

In order to get the most out of *FlashPoint: Ignite Your Potential!*, I suggest you do the following:

1. Take a moment to look over the contents to familiarize yourself with the subject matter.
2. Recognize that several chapters build on, or work with, information in previous ones, so reading the book and doing the exercises in their written order is ideal. However, you can certainly read the book in whatever order you want, since you may have certain subjects that are of greater interest to you.
3. Take advantage of the useful tools provided that will help you learn the information you'll read much more quickly.
4. As you read, think about how you can apply each lesson to your own life.
5. Enjoy the process.

FlashPoint

Are You Aware?

When you finish this chapter, you'll:

◆ Understand how something as simple as personal awareness dramatically affects your life.
◆ Know what *FlashPoints* are and what they can do for you.
◆ Know what knowledge really is and how you can make it work for you.

Awareness Is the First Step

Look around you right now. Look really carefully. Is there anything you just noticed? Something you've never seen before? A mark or crack on the wall? A dent or scuff in the floor? A branch on a tree?

Now listen to the sounds around you. There are probably several sounds happening at the same time. A clock ticking perhaps. Birds chirping or people talking. The sound of traffic. The wind. Some music. Were you paying attention to all of the sounds before?

Okay, where are your hands or feet right now? Do you feel any sensation you may not have noticed a second ago? The fabric or frame of the sofa or chair perhaps? The softness of the carpeting or cool hardness of the floor? The way the binder of this book is trying to close while you hold it open? Were you paying attention to those things before I mentioned them?

If you are like most people, you go through each day exposed to a wide variety of sights, sounds, and other things your senses pick up that I'll bet you pretty much take for granted. You don't always consciously notice them, but if I ask you to notice them, as I just did, you will see, hear, or feel things you might not have noticed before.

"Watch" a Movie Versus "See" a Movie

When you watch a movie at the local theater, you leave the cinema with a certain impression of the film. Your understanding of the film is based on what you saw or noticed while watching it.

If you were to watch the same film a second time, you'd probably notice something you didn't see the first time you watched it. You'd see some new detail or some new element of the plot, because you'd be less focused on finding out "what happens next."

Suppose the next day after seeing the film twice, you run into a friend who saw the same movie, and suppose he asks you if you noticed a certain detail in the flick—and you hadn't. Your friend tells you about a certain scene where there was an obvious error in the editing. It shows the main character with his sleeves rolled up from one camera angle, but they're not rolled up from another. You think to yourself how odd it is that, although you were watching the movie, you didn't "see" that particular detail.

Curious about that detail, you go back and watch the movie a third time. This time you are consciously looking for the detail your friend referred to and, sure enough, you see it just as your friend described it. The main character clearly has his sleeves rolled up, but when the camera angle changes, his sleeves are not rolled up.

I'm sure you'll agree that if you were ever to watch that movie again, you'd notice that tiny little detail every single time. That's because once you become aware of something, it becomes easy to notice and recognize.

Here's the main thought. You could have watched that same movie a dozen times and still not have noticed the editing error, but because your friend brought that detail to your attention, you knew what to look for and saw it clearly.

Guess what: life works in exactly the same way.

Throughout your life you'll have all kinds of opportunities that can help you gain important insights or knowledge. When that happens, you'll understand something in a way that you never noticed or understood it before. You'll "see" it, and you'll never look at "it" (the situation, relationship, or whatever) the "old" way again.

Hitting *FlashPoint*

When you notice or learn something that changes the way you look at things, you've achieved what can be referred to as a realization. If you prefer fancier words, you can call it an epiphany, an awakening, or a revelation. But noticing something is only half the battle.

When you take what you've realized a step further and actually use that information to do something, you've achieved an even more powerful level. I refer to those moments of realization and the corresponding action taken as a *FlashPoint*.

In everyday terms a *FlashPoint* is the lowest temperature at which something will ignite or burn. As it pertains to learning, a *FlashPoint* begins to happen when you say to yourself, "Oh, wow, now I get it!" It's like a light bulb has been turned on. We've all experienced it.

Likewise if you've ever lit a match, you know that simply lighting the match is not enough. In order for the match to do you any good, it will have to continue to burn so that you can do something with it. It's the combination of the match igniting and the match continuing to burn (or continuing to do something with the energy it has created) that results in a true *FlashPoint*.

One of my main objectives in writing this book is to help you recognize important insights that will help you get more out of life, but it doesn't stop there. I want to help you convert those insights into *FlashPoints* whereby you take meaningful action on what you learn—action that can help you get the results you want. If we can accomplish that, you will achieve many more of your wants, wishes, and dreams sooner than you normally would. That means you can accelerate, or speed up, your overall rate of success in life.

The sooner you learn to recognize and use the principles discussed in this book, the sooner you can take advantage of them and make them work for you.

Throughout this book I'll point out potential *FlashPoints* to you. To do so, I'll use the following symbol whenever there is a key idea or thought you should pay special attention to. It may seem like a hokey way to get your attention, but my objective is just that. I want you to notice the important points in this book. I want you to "get it."

FlashPoint =

It's no secret that you can find a treasure much faster if you know where to look and what to look for, but if you want to actually get to the treasure, you also need to start digging for it. The same concept applies to the treasure trove of knowledge in life.

Please go to page 171 in your *Making Connections: Plug-It-In and Work-It-Out Tool Kit* and you'll find something called "My *FlashPoints* Log." It's a handy tool you can use to keep records of the new things you realize or learn . . . if that's something you'd like to do. By keeping a record of your *FlashPoints* as they occur to you, you'll have a summary of insights you can refer to whenever you want to refresh your memory. By noting the date of each *FlashPoint* as well, you'll also have a living record of your personal growth. If you already keep a personal journal, feel free to capture your *FlashPoints* there instead. Of course you can also print out a copy of the log page by going to www.EveryAdvantage.net.

So What Comes Next? Good Question

Imagine that you're leading a wagon train in the Old West. As a responsible wagon master, you have the job of planning the route you take and looking out for the safety of the people traveling with you. You'd probably send a scout to see what's up ahead, and the scout would report his findings back to you. That would enable you to plan the best possible route for the trip. Likewise what we're going to do now is start to look ahead and learn how to plan for, and deal with, what lies ahead of you in life.

We'll start with a short story.

Start by Making Sure You Stay on Course

Two astronauts, a man and a woman, blasted off from Earth on a journey to the moon roughly 240,000 miles away. Going to the moon was always something they wanted to do. It was their "dream" job.

A few hours after take-off the spaceship veered ever so slightly off course.

In the excitement of the space flight, the astronauts were so busy paying attention to other duties that they didn't even realize they had gone slightly off course. At this point in the mission they could still see the moon where it was "supposed" to be when they looked out the spaceship's porthole. Everything seemed okay. Nothing they noticed gave them any reason to believe they were beginning to drift off course, and Mission Control said nothing.

Several hours later the spaceship went even further off course . . . just a little bit. A tiny little bit. By this point something didn't feel right to the astronauts, but they could still see part of the moon out of the porthole, so they continued to rocket through space not realizing they were going further and further away from their intended destination. You see, it was easier for them to just keep going rather than to deal with researching the potential problem. They figured that things would simply work out.

Some of the people at Mission Control told the astronauts everything was okay. Others said they should steer left, and others said right. Unsure about what to do, they just kept going, convincing themselves that everything would work out.

Later the astronauts started to get an even stronger feeling that maybe things weren't really as they should be, but they couldn't put their finger on exactly what the problem might be. At that point someone from Mission Control told them to abort the mission. Someone else told them to keep going. Some said speed up while others instructed them to slow down. So again the astronauts, confused by the many different opinions from the various "experts" at Mission Control, didn't do anything to get back on course. They knew, or at least thought, that Mission Control had more information than they did. Not sure what to do, they just kept going.

A few hours later the spaceship went further off course once again, and then again. By that time the astronauts realized that something was seriously wrong. Things clearly didn't feel right, but since they hadn't corrected the problem earlier when doing so would have been relatively easy, they now knew that reaching the moon (their dream) was no longer possible. So their attention shifted away from the original intention of the flight. They were now forced to focus on other important things . . . like survival.

The astronauts had to abort the intended space mission and managed to steer the spaceship back to Earth. At least on Earth they knew where they were and what to expect. It was safe.

So what does this story tell us? Ask any adult in his or her mid-thirties or beyond what this story means to them. Chances are you'll learn that the story is an analogy for what happens in life to many, if not most, people.

We start our lives having a pretty good idea of where we want to go. As a matter of fact, some experts say that at some level we realize what our real purpose in life is (e.g., our passion) between the ages of 10 and 14 years. We may not think of it in those terms, but early in life we certainly know what we enjoy and what interests us.

As we get older however, we are constantly influenced by a variety of outside forces like peer pressure, parents, teachers, advertisements, and the opinions of other people. We constantly run into obstacles that can derail our progress in the pursuit of our passion, so, over time, a lot of people end up doing something with their lives that is completely different from what they felt or "knew" was the right thing for them when they were younger and, like the astronauts, they end up off course.

Sometimes life's confusion throws people so far off course they can't even remember what they wanted to do with their life in the first place. Then they end up walking through life unhappy and unfulfilled but are unable to put their finger on exactly why they feel that way.

So That's the Way It Is, Huh?

You may remember the Charles Dickens novel, *The Christmas Carol,* in which Scrooge asked the Ghost of Christmas Future, "Spirit, is this the way it will be for me, or is this just the way it could be?" Scrooge later understood that the answer to that question was that you can make life any way you want it, but you've got to be clear about what you want and be committed to achieving it.

Scrooge learned that he could dramatically change the outcome of his life by simply doing things differently and thinking differently.

Young adults often have a certain sense of invulnerability, like nothing can hurt them. Ironically you may also have a sense of insecurity about yourself, who you are, and where life will take you. All of these feelings are normal, but the insecurity and uncertainty you feel can cause you to experience some confusion and doubt that can get you off course, if you allow it to. But only if you allow it to.

As we finish this chapter, remember that knowledge and desire alone will take you only so far in life. Contrary to the popular slogan "knowledge is power," knowledge is not power. Knowledge is like a gallon of gasoline. It's pretty much worthless unless it's used for something, but it can provide tremendous power when used to run an engine. So knowledge is only a potential source of power waiting to be used. To make knowledge valuable, you must actually use it.

Taking responsible action as you become aware of your circumstances is what it will take for you to achieve your goals and dreams. Keep reading and you'll become much more prepared to take specific actions that will help you achieve whatever level of success you choose.

Review

1. To act consciously on something, first you must be aware of it.
2. A *FlashPoint* occurs when you realize something and then take action on it.
3. You can make life any way you want it, but you've got to be clear about what you want and be committed to achieving it.
4. Knowledge is only a potential source of power waiting to be used.

Success and Failure:
What Really Are They?

When you finish this chapter, you'll:

- Be able to define what "success" means to you.
- Recognize the difference between "failure" and "failing."
- Know why some failing is good.
- Understand how you feel about "success" and "failing."
- Be able to define more clearly the results you want to achieve.

I'm sure you hear the word *success* used all the time. Your parents, teachers, friends, and even the media talk about this *success* thing. But what does the word *success* really mean, and does it mean the same thing to everybody?

In this chapter you'll develop your very own, personal definition of *success*. In defining success and what it means to you, you'll gain some very important insights that will help you crystallize, or make clear to you, exactly what you want to achieve.

The fact is that success and failure mean different things to different people. That's why it's important that you clearly define what you think "success" is as well as what you think "failure" is. Once you do that, you'll have a much easier time evaluating your own progress because you'll have a clear picture of what your "success" is supposed to look like.

So Who Exactly Is "Successful"?

Let's start this chapter by looking at a few situations:

◆ Andrea has earned the lead role in her school play and has received a drama scholarship to a top university. To accomplish these things, she has had to stab a number of people in the back, so to speak, and tell a few lies on the way. Is Andrea a success?

◆ David makes $250,000 a year as a doctor and has a large investment portfolio. He owns his own medical practice and drives a foreign luxury automobile. However David is 60 pounds overweight with high blood pressure, his kids don't talk to him, and he has few personal friends. Is David a success?

◆ Derek is a senior in college and is from a poor family. He works weekends as a bag boy at the local grocery store to help his family get along financially. In his spare time he tutors children who have reading disabilities at the local YMCA and has been recognized for his community service. Is Derek a success?

I'm sure that after reading these three scenarios, you've found that success is a term that can mean different things. In other words, success is not a single outcome or condition.

A person can have what seems to be success in one area of life while failing in another. That makes it pretty hard to label someone as an overall *success* in life, doesn't it?

In the next few pages of *FlashPoint* you'll lay the foundation for your personal definition of success. Once you do that, you'll have a much clearer idea about the things you need to accomplish to feel successful personally.

Before we move on, please take a moment right here and list the names of 5 people whom you consider successful. Just list whoever comes to mind when you think of the word *successful:*

Note: If this book belongs to someone else or is a library book, please do this exercise on a separate sheet of paper.

1. _____

2. _____

3. _____

4. _____

5. _____

What made these people come to mind when you thought of the word *successful?* What traits do these 5 people have in common? Jot them down below.

Common traits: _____

_____

So What Exactly Is "Success"?

Ask 50 different people to define success and you'll get as many different answers. At the same time most people will have to think for a minute before they can give you what seems to be a logical answer. That's because very few people take the time to define what success actually means to them. Could that be one reason why so few people ever consider themselves truly successful?

Here's a question for you: If you can't clearly define what success means to you, how will you know what to pursue? How will you ever know if you're successful? Sure, you may feel it when you "get there," but how will you get there if you don't know where "there" is?

So what's your definition of success? How do you know if you're successful? What are your rules for success?

From my research and workshops with young adults I've heard success described in a lot of different ways, including:

- ◆ "Success is personal happiness."
- ◆ "Success is achieving one's personal goals."
- ◆ "Success is giving something your all."
- ◆ "Success is recognition for your work from others."
- ◆ "Success is feeling fulfilled by your accomplishments."

In a moment you'll use a tool that will help you begin to define what success means to you. This will be your first opportunity to come up with your own definition of success. You need to do this for one very important reason:

Once you define what success "looks like" to you, you'll have a clearer picture of exactly what you are trying to achieve. It may not be an exact picture yet (we'll be working on that more later), but having a clearer image of what success means to you will make it a lot easier for you to plan your life so you move toward those things you think of as success. If you are going to "paint a picture" of the outcomes you want in your life, you need to know something about what you want that picture to look like. It just makes sense.

By developing your definition(s) of success early in life, you will be able to compare those definitions with the personal goals you'll set. That way you can ensure that your goals are in line with how you describe success. Once you do that, you're half way to achieving your goals since you'll already be pointed in the right direction.

Now it's your turn to define what success means to you. Please go to page 173 in your *Making Connections: Plug-It-In and Work-It-Out Tool Kit* or log onto www.EveryAdvantage.net to find a short exercise called "My Success." Try your best to complete as much of the exercise as possible. You can always come back and change things later if you want.

What Works for You?

Now that you've had a chance to think about what success means to you, the next step is to learn how to define success in a way that will empower you. We'll explore the difference between *success* and *failure*, and we'll look at how you can set your own rules to determine exactly how you are doing in life.

Let's start by looking at the successes, or failings, of some well-known people.

Albert Einstein was the guy who created the "Theory of Relativity," which led to the nuclear age. By all accounts he is probably the best-known physicist ever. Was Einstein successful? Before you answer that question, did you know that Einstein was four years old before he could speak and seven years old before he could read?

Though Oprah Winfrey was abused as a child, her strong character and intelligence prevailed. Now Oprah is among the most powerful and wealthy people in show business. Is Oprah a success? Was she always?

George "Babe" Ruth is the legendary baseball player who held the record for the most major league career home runs for much of the 20th century until Henry ("Hank") Aaron broke the record in 1974. Was Babe Ruth successful? Before you answer that question, consider that, along the way to setting his record for home runs, Ruth also held the record for the most major league strikeouts. Did that make him a failure?

Abraham Lincoln was the sixteenth, and perhaps one of the greatest, presidents in U.S. history. However Lincoln lost no fewer than 6 elections as he came up in his political career. Did that make him a success or a failure?

Walt Disney founded one of the most successful entertainment companies in the world, and Henry Ford created one of the largest automobile companies in the world. But did you know that both had declared personal bankruptcy before they rose to their higher levels of achievement? And get this. A newspaper editor once fired Walt Disney because he had "no good ideas." Were Disney and Ford successful?

Composer Joseph Haydn (pronounced "Hi-din), one of the greatest composers ever in his own right, gave up making a musician out of his student Ludwig Von Beethoven, who seemed to be "a slow and plodding young man with no apparent talent except his belief in music." Would you consider Beethoven a success? Was Haydn a failure for not recognizing Beethoven's talent?

Each of these stories makes one point perfectly clear. All of these people would now be considered successful in life by almost any standard, yet they each had their share of *failings*. At some point in each of their lives other people might have seen them as failures. Nonetheless each person reached the highest level of achievement in his or her respective field.

So although each of these people experienced some level of success, the question is, "Were they always successful?"

If you believe that success is just a single outcome, a single destination at which one must arrive, then these people weren't always successful. However if you believe that success is a process or a *journey*, we could say that each of their failings taught them something and moved them in the right direction. Each of them learned valuable lessons from his or her mistakes and experiences, and those lessons were needed to help him or her achieve greater things later. So even though each person had their share of what might be considered failings early on, we can say that each person was always in "the process of being successful."

Go Ahead and Fail!

The way we learn to do many things in life is by learning what not to do. As a young child you learned not to touch the stove burner when it's on. Even if you did touch it and burned your fingers, you *successfully learned* not to touch the burner again. So was touching the burner a personal "failing" or was it a successful learning experience? Or could it have been both?

When you started learning how to read, you probably mispronounced many words. Someone (your mom, dad, teacher, etc.) corrected your mistake and told you how to pronounce the word correctly. From mispronouncing the word, you learned both how not to pronounce the word while at the same time learning how to pronounce it correctly. Was mispronouncing the word a failing of yours or a successful learning experience? Or could it have been both?

Earl Nightingale was one of the best-known American thinkers on the subject of success. He described success this way: "Success is the progressive realization of a worthy ideal." What Nightingale meant is that success is a journey rather than a destination, or put another way, success is a "process."

Nightingale's definition says that you are successful as long as you are moving in the right direction. This definition of success is excellent since it makes it very difficult not to be successful. As long as you are moving in the right direction, you are in the "process" of being successful.

I define success in a similar way.

Success is the process of doing the right things, in the right way in order to move you toward the achievement of worthwhile personal goals. Let's break this definition down a bit.

Doing the Right *Things*

If success is about doing the right things in the right way, then what exactly are the "right things"?

The right things are, quite simply, anything that supports your personal values and is necessary to move you closer to achieving a meaningful personal goal. Clearly something can't possibly be the right thing for you to do if it doesn't support your personal values. That just wouldn't make sense. It wouldn't be "right."

At the same time keep in mind that the right things may not always be things you want to do. Here are some examples of what I mean.

> 66 **In life the way we learn to do many things is by learning what not to do.** 99

- ◆ Getting on your bicycle and falling down a number of times in order to learn how to ride it. Falling may not feel good, but it may be necessary to help you learn how to ride your bike correctly.

- ◆ Cutting out eating things you really like in order to achieve a goal of losing weight. Giving up your favorite junk foods might not be pleasant, but it would be the right thing to do to achieve your goal.

- ◆ Spending a lot of time doing homework so you can earn a good grade in class. If doing well in that class is an important goal of yours, it may be necessary to spend more time studying and less time "playing."

- Breaking up with someone you care about whom you know is not right for you. We both know that would be a hard thing to do, but if it is the right thing to do, you may have to do it.

As these examples show, doing the right thing in order to achieve your goals may involve some degree of either failing or discomfort, but if that experience of failing or discomfort moves you closer to achieving a worthwhile personal goal, or if it creates a valuable learning experience for you, then it is probably the right thing for you to do.

Doing Things in the Right Way

Doing things in the right way involves the same two principles as doing the right things.

First, doing something in the "right way" means doing something in a manner that moves you closer to achieving your personal goal. Secondly, something can be done in the right way only if the action is in line with your personal values. If the way you accomplish something doesn't support your values, then you are not doing what is right for you. Again let's look at some examples.

- Going back to our last example, let's say you're a student and you want to do well in a certain class. If your goal is to "do well" in that class, but you cheat on the tests, are you successful? The answer to that question goes back to your personal values. In this case the question would be, "Do you see honesty and integrity as more important values than deception and dishonesty?"

In other words ask yourself, "Is the process by which I got the good grade in class (in this case by cheating) consistent with my personal value system?" If it isn't, you wouldn't truly be successful, even if your outcome is an "A" in the class.

- What if your goal is to own a really cool jacket you saw in the store. If you decide to take a shortcut and use what we'll call a "five-finger discount" to steal the jacket, would you successfully own the jacket or would you have an item that doesn't really belong to you? Again you'd need to look at your personal values to make that decision. It's your call.

In short you can be successful at something only if it is the right thing for you to do and you do it in a way that is consistent with your personal values, i.e., the right way.

Failing vs. Failure

When you think of the word *fail,* you probably drum up the image of doing something unsuccessfully. Failing has a negative meaning attached to it because it's usually perceived that failing at something is, in some way, a sign of weakness. However, the truth is that failing, in and of itself, is not necessarily a bad thing. In fact it can be a very good thing. Let's look at why.

Take riding a bicycle again. When you first learned how to ride a bicycle (assuming you have), you probably fell down a couple of times.

Does the fact that you fell (probably more than one time) mean you were a failure at riding a bike? Of course not. In fact you needed to fail in order to learn what not to do—in order to learn how not to ride your bike. And because of that, once you learned what not to do, at the same time you learned more about what you needed to do in order to stay up and ride successfully.

The fact is that the most successful people on Earth are also the most consistent failers. Hold on, does that sound right? Yes, it's right. The most successful people are not failures, mind you, but rather failers, a subtle difference that means a whole lot.

Successful people keep doing something until they get it right. They are persistent and are willing to fail in order to learn and grow. I'm not saying that failing is fun, but successful people tolerate failing as necessary in the learning process and in the process of achieving success. I'm sure you'll agree that when people are afraid to fail at something, they often won't even try doing it in the first place.

Sure. **It's a fact that if you don't try to do something you can't fail at it, but at the same time you can't succeed at it either.** We'll talk more about the fear of failure later on.

Given that obvious fact, which do you think is worse: to act and fail at something or to fail to act at all? Consider that when you act and fail, you at least learn something, but if you never even try to do something, you are no better off at all, because you have neither succeeded nor learned something by failing. Face it. Unless you try to do something, you're virtually *guaranteed* that you can never be successful at doing it.

Successful Failing:
The Oxymoron for Smart People

There is a clear difference between being a failure and simply failing at something. Failing helps you learn. Failing is a necessary part of life. If you don't fail, you don't learn, and if you don't learn, you don't grow.

As discussed already, if you are learning to ride your bike and you fall, you have failed only at that single attempt to ride the bike. At that very moment you would be a successful failer and not an unsuccessful failure. That's because you'd simply get up and try to ride the bike again.

Your success in this situation is that you would have learned at least one way not to ride the bike. You learned something.

> **❝ The fact is that the most successful people on Earth are also the most consistent failers. ❞**

Now it's a completely different story if you fall down on your bike and decide you will never try to ride it again because you don't want to fail. If that were the situation, you *would* be a failure at riding your bike because you had the opportunity to learn to do so and gave up.

Again I'm not saying that failing feels good. Obviously there are more pleasant feelings. What I am saying is that failing is a necessary part of the learning process, so realize now that it's okay to have some failings. In order to succeed you will almost always need to fail first.

Remember this: **As long as you keep trying to do or to learn something, you cannot be a failure at it.** If you have the ability and the will to try again, you cannot be a failure because "it" isn't over yet. *You cannot be a failure at something until you give up trying.* Until you give up trying, there is still a chance for you to achieve the outcome you want.

Thomas Watson, the former chief executive officer of IBM, once said, "If you want to increase your success rate, double your failure rate." Let's change that statement just a little bit and say, "The way to succeed is to double your *failing* rate." We'll take a closer look at why that's true in the next chapter.

The truth is that a person who never makes a mistake rarely achieves anything of value. That's because everything in life is relative. In other words we need to understand what is wrong in order to know what is right. Without light, there is no dark. Without up, there is no down. Without hot, there is no cold. Without young, there is no old. Without mistakes and failing, there is no "success." Everything is relative.

The key difference between successful people and those whom we call failures is that successful people try again at least one more time than failures do. Think about it. Successful people keep trying to achieve their objectives, while failures simply give up.

I have an acronym I use for the word failure. **F.A.I.L.U.R.E.** means "Final Attempt In Life Under Reasonable Expectations." That is, a failure is someone who simply stops trying when there is a reasonable chance he still can succeed. To put it another way, if you keep trying to accomplish something, you are not a failure at it.

So you'll never be a failure unless you give up trying to achieve a worthwhile personal goal.

But . . . Know When to Quit

You might be thinking, "I can't imagine that I should always keep trying forever? Sometimes I think I'd be better off not trying any more," and you'd be right.

Although success means we keep moving toward the achievement of a worthwhile personal goal, sometimes you do need to know when simply to stop at something and cut your losses.

That's what I mean by "under reasonable expectations" because there are times when expectations for success are unreasonable and where not trying any more makes more sense than to keep trying.

One example might be if you were to try to hold your breath for two days. In that case a reasonable expectation would tell most people to stop trying after they master about two to three minutes without taking a breath. It would be unfair to say that you are a failure at holding your breath for two days because that expectation is not a reasonable one. That's a radical example, but you get the point.

Just know that there will be certain things in life you will not be successful at. Nobody can be successful at everything. But there is a difference between quitting at something when you've tried many times to achieve it and recognize that there is no way to be successful at it and quitting because you are simply tired of trying or are afraid of failing. The bottom line is this: if your objective is truly worthwhile and you believe there is a chance you can succeed, then you should keep trying to achieve it. But be intelligent as you try.

Don't Be Insane

Here's what I mean by "be intelligent as you try." If your attempt to succeed at something isn't working, you need to examine what you're doing and how you're going about doing it. In other words your own actions may be keeping you from getting the result you want. I'm sure you'll agree that it would be insane to keep doing the same thing over and over in the same exact way if it isn't working for you.

They say that the Chinese definition of insanity is, "Doing what you've always done in exactly the same way and expecting a different outcome." Do you know anybody who does that?

Here's a way to look at it. Professional marketing people know how this works when it comes to advertising. If a successful advertising agency runs an ad and it doesn't work, they don't run the same ad again and again hoping it will work. Instead they change the ad in some way, test the ad in another publication, or create a completely new ad and run that one instead.

Guy Finley, author of *The Secret of Letting Go—The Effortless Path to Inner Success,* says, "Defeat comes from clinging to solutions that don't work." My personal point of view on the subject is, "If you keep doing exactly what you're doing, you'll keep getting exactly what you're getting."

So if you want to change the results you are getting, you should consider changing the way you are going about trying to get the result.

One of my neighbors tries to teach his dog to come to him by hitting the animal if it doesn't come when he calls it. Would you come to someone you thought might hit you? Of course not. And yet my neighbor continues to do something that doesn't work, again and again, hoping he'll get a different result.

I've got news for him. If he keeps doing what he's doing, he'll keep getting the same results he's getting. The dog will never come on a consistent basis if he hits it when it finally does come.

Are you doing anything over and over in the same way and hoping to get a different result? The way you study perhaps? Maybe the way you're approaching someone you like but aren't getting the reaction you want? Or maybe you have a diet that you're trying over and over just because you heard it "should" work.

If something isn't working for you, you may want to try doing something else to get the result you're seeking.

Please go to page 175 in your *Making Connections: Plug-It-In and Work-It-Out Tool Kit,* or log onto www.EveryAdvantage.net and you'll find an exercise called "Results I Want." It can help you think through how to get better results at almost anything you want to accomplish.

Success Takes Work

Jim Herrick, former head coach of the UCLA Bruins championship basketball team, put it well when he said, "The only place you'll find 'success' before 'work' is in the dictionary."

That's a great phrase, but it's also very true. Remember, the definition of success includes doing the right things. Doing means you must work at achieving your goal. You must do something.

Virtually *all* worthwhile achievements are going to involve a certain amount of work. Now when I say work, I don't necessarily mean something that is hard and unpleasant. Rather, "work" means taking some action that moves you closer to your goal and moves your goal closer to you. It means doing something to attract the result you want.

Here's another way to think about it. Success or failure is a condition that you draw to yourself based on what you do and what you are able to achieve.

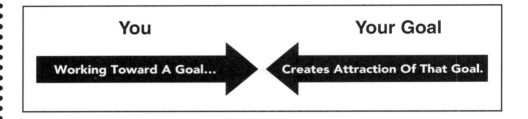

You — Working Toward A Goal... Your Goal — Creates Attraction Of That Goal.

Let's say you consider having money to be a sign of success, and many people do. In order to get that money, you need to provide something of value to whomever is paying you in order to draw the money to you. Let's face it. If you could get money without having to add any value, you would just be handed all the money you wanted, right? But life doesn't work that way. If others are paying you, you need to offer them some form of value so that the money is given (attracted) to you. It works the same way for attracting virtually any result.

When professional athletes become really good at what they do, the scouts seek them out. The finest basketball player in the world doesn't have to go chase pro teams. Rather those teams will be chasing (will be drawn to) him or her. That's because the basketball player has worked to become good at the game, and in turn has *attracted* the desired result.

Likewise the finest schools seek out the best students. The best companies pursue the best employees. The best hospitals go after the best doctors and nurses for their staff. The most discriminating art collectors and museums chase the work of the best artists.

Each of the above situations indicates that success is drawn to each individual like a magnet. You are not drawn to success. Instead you draw success to you by accomplishing something . . . by doing something . . . by being something. Likewise if you decide just to stand still and do nothing and hope that success comes your way, you can be successful only at one thing: standing still and doing nothing. Literally nothing will be drawn to you (except maybe some dust).

Albert Einstein once said, "Don't aim to become a person of success. Aim to become a person of value." The way to become a person of value is to do and learn the things that increase your value to yourself or to others. So, if you are a person of value, success will be drawn to you, but you can only be successful at something if you consistently strive to achieve it.

> **❝ If you just stand still and do nothing, you can be successful at only one thing: standing still and doing nothing. ❞**

I really want you to absorb this concept. **A "success" is not something you become. Rather it is something you attract to yourself by what you do and by who you are as a person.**

You Don't Need to Reinvent the Wheel

Some people think that in order to be successful they need to be an innovator and come up with another way of doing things that nobody else has thought of, but that's not necessarily true. Creating new things and new methods can certainly help you succeed, but as business philosopher Jim Rohn puts it, "To be successful you don't have to do extraordinary things; just do ordinary things extraordinarily well."

Walt Disney once described the way to become financially successful as simply opening up the yellow pages of a telephone book, picking a type of business, and finding a way to provide that product or service better than others do. And Walt walked his talk.

Walt Disney had the idea of opening an amusement park. At the time amusement parks were known to be dirty and dangerous places to go, but Disney wanted to take an ordinary thing like the amusement park and make it an extraordinary experience, and Disneyland® was born.

Automobiles were once assembled one single car at a time until Henry Ford came up with a better way of doing an ordinary thing. He invented the manufacturing assembly line, and the rest is manufacturing history.

Movies were never the same once Stephen Spielberg came onto the scene and made *Close Encounters of the Third Kind* and *E.T. The Extra Terrestrial*. George Lucas made a similar impact when he brought the first *Star Wars*® movie to the big screen in the late 1970s. Both of these directors took the art of filmmaking and special effects to new heights by taking the ordinary concept of making a movie and doing extraordinary things with it.

> **66 To be successful you don't have to do extraordinary things; just do ordinary things extraordinarily well. 99**
>
> **—Jim Rohn**

Bill Gates, perhaps the most successful software entrepreneur in the world and a founder of Microsoft® Corporation, is a software legend. Although he didn't invent the concept of software, I'm sure you'll agree he's done extraordinary things with it. Gates knew that it wasn't the hardware of the computer that added the value but rather the software. So he took the concept of software development to new heights until his operating system dominated the PC market.

Debbie Fields, founder of Mrs. Fields Cookies®, took the ordinary concept of cookies and became successful by opening stores that sold just cookies, something that had never been done on a large scale before. She is a millionaire many times over because she figured out how to make and market an ordinary item like cookies in an extraordinary way.

Starbucks® sells coffee, Wal-Mart® is a discount store chain, McDonald's® sells hamburgers, and so on. None of these businesses invented its industry. Each business simply took its industry to new heights by doing ordinary things in extraordinary ways.

Mother Theresa took public service leadership to a new level as did

Martin Luther King Jr., Caesar Chavez, and Mahatma Gandhi. Michael Jordan, Michelle Kwan, Nancy Lopez, Sheryl Swoops, Nolan Ryan, Roberto Clemente, Wayne Gretzke, and Walter Payton reached the top of their respective sports by outperforming their peers. Abraham Lincoln, Winston Churchill, and Nelson Mandela took political leadership to new heights. And the lists go on and on.

You can reach the same level of achievement with your success goals. Your process of *doing the right things in the right way* should include trying to be the best you can be at whatever you decide to do. Once you're the best, all that's left is all the rest!

Don't Just Try to Try

It can be easy to fake yourself out on your success journey by convincing yourself you are taking action when you really aren't. This sort of thing often takes place when people use the term "I'll try" in place of actually doing something.

Simply saying you'll try to do something is not enough. Saying "I'll try" can be confused by your subconscious with actually doing something, but I'm sure you'll admit that it doesn't get the same result.

I once heard that high achievers use the term "I'll try" an average of once per day, while low achievers use the same term an average of eight times per day. That's because low achievers somehow associate saying that they'll "try" with the actual action of doing. But saying and doing are not the same thing. If you say you are going to try to do something, you won't get anywhere unless you actually follow through with action.

In the real world nobody gives a hoot when you say you'll try something unless you actually follow through and keep your word. They'll be impressed only if they actually "see" you try. So be prepared to do something other than simply say you'll try.

It's true that if you don't do something you can't fail at it, but you can't succeed either. Like they used to say in the old Nike® commercials, "Just do it™".

Fear of Failure

Why do you think babies continue to try to walk even though they fall down over and over as they try? There are several answers to that question. We can learn a lot from babies.

First, babies don't see falling as failure. They don't judge things in that way. Babies don't consider the option of failure (giving up) because they haven't learned to be afraid of it . . . yet.

Second, babies have a strong drive to succeed. They are naturally programmed with the tools (legs and a balancing system) and attitude (the desire to go faster) that compel them to try to walk.

Third, babies don't care what others will think of them if they fail at something. In contrast most adults constantly live in fear of their own self-criticism, and they worry about what others think of them to boot. It is this fear of looking bad to others, or to one's self, which keeps many people from even trying to do certain things.

> **❝ It is this fear of looking bad to others, or to one's self, which keeps many people from even trying to do certain things. ❞**

I remember when I went downhill skiing for the first time with a college girlfriend. She brought me to a ski resort in Wisconsin where the ski slopes ranged in difficulty from "bunny" hills, or easy slopes, all the way up to hills for advanced skiers, which I certainly was not.

We brought my girlfriend's little brother (we'll call him Bob) with us on that trip. He was probably four or 5 years younger than I was, and it was his first time skiing just as it was mine.

By the end of the day Bob was able to get down some of the intermediate hills gracefully. I, on the other hand, couldn't even get down the easiest slopes without having to fall on my butt to stop at the bottom of the hill. I was older, bigger, and stronger than that little dude, yet he developed much more quickly as a skier than I did. Why do you think that happened?

Here's what happened. At the beginning of the day Bob was smart enough to take a couple of quick lessons from the local ski instructor on the bunny hill. The lessons were free, and he took advantage of this.

I was not so smart. Instead I thought to myself, "Hey, I'm a senior in college. I will absolutely not embarrass myself (fail) by being seen on the bunny hill taking lessons." So instead I went directly up the ski lift and started my first run down the amateur hill. Well, guess what? I couldn't figure out how to steer the skis, much less stop. So I ended up rocketing down the hill at what must have been 50 miles per hour only to realize three hundred feet from the bottom that I'd better just sit down or I'd end up running into a small creek.

Throughout the day I thought I could go back up the hill and get a little better each time I came down. And although I did improve in a minor way, I still couldn't gracefully stop at the bottom of the hill by the end of the day. I just didn't know how.

The irony is that in an effort to not look uncool (failing in my eyes) by taking lessons on the bunny hill, I looked totally stupid all day as I fell on my rump to stop each and every time. Meanwhile by the end of the day Bob was becoming a comfortable skier, and I winced each time he rubbed in how much better at it he was than me.

So what messed me up in this situation? It was my *fear of failure*. In other words it was my fear that others would see me as uncool or inexperienced (on the bunny hill) that made me not even try to get any help learning how to ski.

Bob, on the other hand, had it right. He had a desire to succeed and didn't care about what others thought as he took lessons. It wasn't even a consideration. His desire to succeed, to learn how to get it right, developed him into a pretty good skier in a single day. As for me, my fear of failure resulted in exactly what I was trying to avoid, namely, looking stupid. Do you know anybody this sort of story might apply to?

If you're like a lot of the students I interviewed for my research, you may have some fear of failure yourself. You might be curious to know that one of the most common fears I hear from young adults is the fear of not accomplishing one's personal goals and dreams. It is exactly that reason that you will be better off if you focus on the . . .

. . . Desire to Succeed

Let's flip sides now and talk about the desire to succeed.

There is a story of two 10-year-old boys who were out playing on an icy lake that was supposed to be frozen solid. One of the little boys happened to step onto a spot where the ice was too thin, and he fell into the water and was immediately pulled under the ice by the current.

His friend started beating on the ice with his foot trying to break it, but it wasn't working. As the boy looked up to see if anyone was around who could help him, he happened to see a tree branch laying on the ground a short distance away. He ran to it and ripped off a branch and quickly came back to try to get his buddy out. The little boy started beating on the ice with the branch over and over and eventually the thick ice cracked, and then shattered, and he pulled his friend out to safety.

When the paramedics arrived, they saw what had happened. The ice was thick and they were baffled by how this little 10-year-old boy could break the ice with a tree branch. It should have been impossible. One of the paramedics even tried beating on the ice himself and couldn't crack it.

An old man standing nearby hearing the conversation approached the paramedics and said, "I'll tell you how he did it. He didn't have anybody here to tell him he couldn't."

This story illustrates an important point. Had the second little boy feared he could not break the ice with the branch he'd found, he wouldn't have even tried to break it out of the expectation that he would fail. Instead the boy's desire to succeed outweighed any fear of failure he may have had and drove him into action to save his friend from drowning.

So the final lesson in this section is that **in order to be successful at anything, you must first start by attempting to do it.** And in order for you to want to do something, your desire to succeed at it must outweigh your fear of failing at it. **Desire will catapult you into taking the actions you need to take. Fear will freeze you into inaction.**

Fear of Success

We've already touched on the fact that sometimes we don't do certain things because of the fear of failing at them. But could it also be that we may avoid doing certain things because we fear succeeding? The answer is a profound "yes!" Fear of success is every bit as real as the fear of failure.

So, why would someone fear success? After all, success is a good thing, isn't it? Let's look at this issue a bit more closely.

If I ask you now what you'd consider personal success, you can probably give me an answer. However, imagine that I then snap my fingers and give you the success you described. Something fundamental has immediately changed, hasn't it? What has changed is that you now need to do something with your newfound success. You now have an additional responsibility to fulfill.

For example, if you think success is all about money and I dump five million dollars on you, all of a sudden you have the responsibility of doing something with that money, with that "success." How would you use it? How would you make sure you don't lose it? How would you invest it? How would you deal with your friends or relatives who either want a loan or want you to give them a large sum of money to start a business? How would you handle calls from charities asking you to give them money?

If you think success means being famous and I snap my fingers and immediately make you a celebrity, would you be prepared to handle the tremendous media attention and the nuisance of crazy fans following you? How would you deal with having incorrect or exaggerated information being printed about you in the tabloids or the constant requests from groups asking you to make free appearances?

Or maybe you think a measure of success is having a family, so I snap my fingers and give you a spouse and three children along with a new mother- and father-in-law. Can you support your new family? Are you prepared for parenthood? For a relationship with a spouse? For dealing with your partner's parents?

Have you ever known someone who really wanted to meet another person, and when he or she finally got the chance to meet that person, he or she said or did something really stupid? Maybe it was an accident, and then maybe it wasn't a total accident.

So truly **wanting success, and having success, are two completely different things**. Wanting success is driven by pure desire for the most attractive parts of the outcome, while having success requires you to deal with all parts of the outcome, good and bad. That takes a great degree of responsibility and discipline once the outcome occurs.

My father was a successful businessman. He owned about a dozen grocery stores with a couple of partners. Then when I was 10 years old, my father's business failed. We quickly went from being financially comfortable to financially struggling. As a young child I saw this incident in a very destructive way. Deep down inside I decided that it might not pay to become financially successful because success can be taken away from you. I feared being financially successful, because I feared losing my success. It took me years to figure that out, but when I did, things really started to go my way.

So as you try to succeed at things and don't seem to be getting the results you want, consider if you aren't getting those results because, at some level, you are actually afraid of what it will mean if you do achieve them. If you do recognize that as the case, you'll be better prepared to manage your emotions to overcome it.

Your Friends and Your Success

Your friends wish you well, don't they? Of course they do, but sometimes they may not want you to do *that* well. Deep down inside I think most people know this, and it can be another reason to fear success.

It's important to understand that once you start becoming more successful at something than others are, you will alienate (or "distance") yourself from people. You won't alienate them by anything bad you've done to them. Instead, some people will feel less significant because you've shown them that success can be achieved. In other words you've shown that "it" can be done.

The fact you've proven that success can be achieved puts a lot of pressure on your friends who now have to look at themselves in the mirror and wonder why they haven't achieved what you have. Envy isn't simply about wanting what another person has. A large part of envy is wondering why *you* don't have what the other person has.

As you move in the direction of success, you need to understand that other people are going to pull away from you because they're terrified that they are not doing enough compared to you.

It's very easy to blame the world when you're not successful. Therefore when you have a friend who's as smart as you, who's as good a person as you, and who's about as educated as you are, who watches you go out there and make something of your life, there is a risk that your friend will be filled with a certain degree of fear and may pull away from the source of that fear, namely, you. It's important that you recognize this and don't allow your fear of others possibly pulling away from you to stop you from achieving your goals.

So being successful is a great thing, but it can also be a very scary thing if you're not prepared to handle it. There are a number of reasons that may make you fearful of success. You simply need to be aware of those reasons and overcome the roadblocks they may cause you.

Please go to page 178 in your *Making Connections: Plug-It-In and Work-It-Out Tool Kit* and you'll find the "Fear of Success Test." You can also find a copy at www.EveryAdvantage.net. It's a short questionnaire you can take to help you determine how much or how little you may fear success.

Review

Now that you've taken the "Fear of Success Test," let's review what we learned in this chapter.

1. I define success as the process of doing the right things, in the right way, that moves you toward the achievement of worthwhile personal goals. You may have developed your own definition by now too.
2. In life the way we learn to do most things is by learning what not to do. We learn through failings.
3. Failing is not the same as being a failure. It is absolutely fine to fail. If we do not fail, we do not learn. As long as you keep trying to do or learn something, you cannot be a failure at it.
4. The key difference between successes and failures is that successful people pick themselves up to try again at least one more time than failures do.
5. Adjust your definition of the word *failure* to mean "Final Attempt In Life Under Reasonable Expectations." By using this as your definition of failure, you'll know that you cannot be a failure unless you simply give up trying to succeed.
6. The Chinese definition of insanity is, "Doing what you've

always done in exactly the same way and expecting a different outcome." So if you aren't getting the results you want, try a *different* way.

7. A success in not something you become. Instead you draw the condition of success to you by creating value.

8. As philosopher Jim Rohn puts it, "To be successful you don't have to do extraordinary things; just do ordinary things extraordinarily well."

9. In order for you to want to do something, your desire to succeed at it must outweigh your fear of failing at it.

10. Fear of success is as real as the fear of failure, and it can sabotage your ability to succeed . . . but only if you let it.

If you'd like to, you can now revisit your definition of *success*—the one you developed earlier in this chapter—to see if your definitions of success and happiness have changed at all. Once you do that, please move on to the next chapter. There are a lot more great things to learn and build on.

Keep On Keepin' On

When you finish this chapter, you'll:

◆ Know why perseverance is a common characteristic of life's greatest achievers.
◆ Understand what procrastination is and why it really occurs.
◆ Have a better understanding of what you will be most likely to persevere at and follow through with.

When I started writing this book, I put a lot of thought into the order in which the chapters needed to be in order to create the most effective learning experience for you. It occurred to me what one subject had to appear early in the book: this one. It isn't a long chapter, but it is just as important, or possibly more so, than any of the others.

So we're going to start with an overview of perhaps the single most important factor that determines one's level of success in life. That factor is perseverance.

What Is Perseverance?

According to Webster's Dictionary, perseverance is defined as "the stead-fast adherence to a course of action, belief or purpose." A similar word to perse-verance is *persistence*. Persistence is defined as "holding steadfastly and firmly to a purpose, state or undertaking despite obstacles, warnings or setbacks."

Both perseverance and persistence are easy concepts to understand. They essentially mean you keep on trying to succeed regardless of what happens. But for a great majority of people the concept of perseverance is difficult to actually do.

In this chapter you'll learn why that's the case. You'll also learn how you can increase your level of success by demonstrating greater perseverance in the things that are important to you.

Those Who Persevere Ultimately Win

One of the single greatest characteristics of high achievers is that they exhibit a strong ability to persevere. In all walks of life it is statistically proven that those who persevere and persist through obstacles are far more likely to achieve what they set out to do than those who tend to give up on things. It makes sense, doesn't it? If you stop trying to accomplish something, you stop making progress, and if you halt your progress, you'll never get to your desired destination.

While perseverance may sound like a simple concept, it isn't necessarily easy to execute, so this chapter of *FlashPoint* will give you the perspective and tools necessary to persevere and follow through on whatever you do.

History is full of examples of people who demonstrated perseverance and persistence to achieve high levels of success. Here are a few examples:

◆ Twenty-one corporations rejected Chester Carlson's device he called a Xerox machine, but Carlson knew what he had. He persisted in marketing the Xerox and the rest is history.

◆ Twenty-eight publishers said, "No, thank you" to

Theodore Geisel's first children's' book. He is also known as Doctor Seuss. Did you ever read Cat in a Hat or any of the other Doctor Seuss publications? Millions upon millions have read and loved those books only because Geisel didn't give up on his attempts to get published.

◆ Colonel Harlan Sanders tried to sell his chicken recipe for years before he was able to finally find a buyer. He knew what the business potential of his creation was and believed in his goal, and eventually KFC (Kentucky Fried Chicken) was born when Sanders was in his 60s.

◆ The international best seller *Jonathan Livingston Seagull*, by Richard Bach, was rejected by dozens of publishers before it finally was accepted for publication. It went on to become one of the best-selling books of all time.

◆ Stories similar to these are seen in all arenas of life. Apartheid survived in South Africa for a long time—until a jailed leader named Nelson Mandela was finally freed after 25 years of fighting apartheid from his jail cell. He didn't quit pursuing his mission. He could have given up, but he didn't.

◆ Comediennes like Whoop Goldberg and Rosie O'Donnell played in smoky nightclubs for years before they finally achieved stardom. They persevered and it paid off big time.

◆ Communism seemed to be a permanent condition in what was once known as the Soviet Union, but certain individuals like Lech Walesa persistently led the fight against communism until it finally began to crumble in the late 1980s. Along with communism fell the wall separating East and West Berlin—a wall that had been up for more than 30 years.

◆ Finally it took me more than 18 years of research and 7 years of writing to complete *FlashPoint*.

The fact is that any "wall" will fall if it is beaten on long enough. In the same way, perseverance is the consistent hammering away at something until it finally happens.

Worthwhile Things Rarely Happen Overnight

As much as we'd like or wish them to, it is rare that anything truly worthwhile can be accomplished overnight. There are exceptions, but the exceptions are usually possible because some groundwork has already been laid for them to happen.

Inventor Thomas Edison once said, "Everything comes to him who waits, but it comes sooner to him who hustles while he's waiting."

People who understand and display perseverance know that the results they want don't always come immediately, so they continue to strive toward their objectives. Their belief in what they do drives them to pursue their objectives until they achieve them.

What Causes Perseverance?

Let's start by putting some perspective on this subject by looking at our formal primary education system. In U.S. schools we are taught that success means getting good grades and doing well in your studies. That's the marker the formal education system emphasizes. It's not a big conspiracy or anything. "Success" in the U.S. education system is simply measured by the grades you get, because grades are easy to measure. Grades are a yardstick for measuring progress.

As students we're told:

◆ "Get good grades to be at the top of your class."
◆ "Do well in school so you can go to a good university or college."

◆ "Get a high grade point average because it looks impressive on your resume."

For the record, I do believe that getting good grades is important. It's important because in striving for them, you develop your thinking skills and other important things like self-discipline.

In the U.S. we often test kids as early as first grade to decide whether they get into "gifted and talented" classes. If they do get in, we label the child as gifted, and if they don't get in, we assume he or she is not. But here's what's so interesting. At an early age the result of a test like this really does nothing more than indicate to what degree the child was academically developed at the time he or she took the test. It won't identify every child who is gifted and it won't exclude every kid who isn't. Certainly some children are truly "gifted," but that's not the point.

Some children simply "catch on" sooner than others. It's what enlightened educators call "developmental." In other words, different kids will develop different aspects of their thinking, motor skills, and even when they get their first tooth at different times.

So we label kids either gifted or not gifted. However, these gifted and talented programs do not necessarily indicate whether the so-called "gifted child" will be successful in life. They only indicate in what areas of thinking (mostly academic) the child has developed to that point. There are a variety of other factors in determining one's likelihood of "success" other than being able to do well on tests or getting good grades.

I know some incredibly intelligent people who are just getting by in life, and I know some less intelligent people who are at the top of their professions. But how can that happen if success is determined by intelligence and grades alone? Maybe there are other factors that come into play, huh? There's no question about it, and one of the key indicators that someone will be successful in life is his or her level of perseverance and persistence in pursuing goals. It's really a mathematical issue. Those who keep trying simply have a better chance of eventually succeeding than those who give up trying.

President Calvin Coolidge stated it well when he said, "Nothing in the world can take the place of persistence. Talent will not. Nothing is more common than unsuccessful men with talent. Genius will not. Unrewarded genius is almost a proverb. Education will not. The world is full of educated derelicts. Persistence and determination alone are omnipotent."

There are many countries, particularly in the Far East, that don't simply focus on academic aspects of students. These educational systems emphasize perseverance and diligent work. They know that the deciding factor in your ability to be successful is just as often how determined you are when you go after something as it is by how intelligent you are.

It's no wonder that so many immigrants from other countries come to the U.S. with nothing and end up owning successful businesses or become successful professionals. They aren't more intelligent than the rest of the population. They simply work at their plans until they achieve their objectives. When you combine perseverance with a strong desire to succeed that outweighs any fear of failure, you've got a winning formula.

In the U.S. we tend to believe that being smart will pay off. Being smart is equated with success. And based on the way our school systems work, being smart is definitely an advantage when it comes to academic measurement.

Meanwhile, many Americans look at immigrants with envy. When you're raised in America, success is "supposed" to be an overnight phenomenon (i.e., winning the lottery, getting good grades every 6 weeks, getting drafted into professional sports directly from high school, etc.), but in reality it usually takes time and diligent work. Many immigrants know this. They grow up with a realistic perspective on what it takes to succeed instead of a "quick-win" mentality, so they develop a plan to achieve their goals and plug away at it persistently until they hit pay dirt.

 These people are no smarter than anyone else except for one thing. **They know that being persistent is just as important as being smart.**

FlashPoint Revisited

People who persevere understand that success is created over time. They know that there is usually a learning, or building, process that needs to occur before they can reach their ultimate objective, or *FlashPoint*. (Remember the Number Hunt exercise?)

If you take a match and waive it a couple of feet over a drop of lighter fluid or gasoline (by the way, obviously I don't want you to do this), the gas vapors will not ignite. The match needs to be closer to the fumes to ignite them.

As the match is moved closer and closer to the combustible liquid it will finally reach a point where it is close enough to the gas vapors that the heat of the match causes the vapors to ignite. You've probably seen this happen when you light your barbecue grill. At this point the flammable substance has hit "ignition."

Life works in exactly the same way. When we first try to do something, we don't often reach the ignition point immediately. However, human beings are often impatient and we tend to look for immediate gratification. So rather than keep trying to achieve our objective, we often quit either far before, or sometimes even right before, "ignition" occurs.

Imagine if your favorite musical artist gave up on composing your favorite song right before he (or she) "figured it out," just because she (or he) got a little frustrated. What a shame that would be.

One fundamental difference between high achievers and lower achievers is that high achievers will continue to pursue a worthwhile objective even after lower achievers would give up trying. Top achievers realize that perseverance is critical to reaching the reward. They know that to keep trying is a fundamental part of the success formula.

One of the best definitions I've ever heard for perseverance is from Jim Rohn, author of *Take Charge of Your Life*. He describes perseverance as "patience in action." I think that definition hits the nail on the head. What it means is that we need to keep doing what we know we need to do with the understanding that it may take some time to achieve the desired result.

The disadvantage we often have when we're younger is that we haven't yet developed a perspective of time. As we get older however, we start to see patterns of how things actually work. We see the benefits of sticking to something, because over time we do stick to certain things until they become a reality. That insight is critical in the development of perseverance. We must understand that the payoff is usually there, waiting for us, if we are willing to stick it out, but we must be genuinely committed to achieving the payoff in order to have the mental energy to persevere.

Commitment to something both causes perseverance and comes from perseverance. If you are committed, you will keep trying, and if you keep trying, you have a vested interest in not giving up.

A person who perseveres keeps trying and may look at different ways of doing something until he gets the results he wants. He takes continuous action to get the result. So perseverance is not so much a matter of what you do or how you do it. It is simply that you keep trying for the desired result, realizing that sometimes things, particularly important things, take time.

Sometimes you need time to learn what doesn't work in order to understand that there may be a better way of doing something (remember failing versus failure).

As I mentioned in the last chapter, in the advertising business an ad agency may run a particular ad. If the ad doesn't work for some reason, they don't totally give up on trying to promote the product or service. Instead they try a different approach to the advertising. Oddly enough, though, some people believe that if they keep doing what they're doing, they'll eventually achieve their objective. Although that can be the case, you need to realize when to change what you're doing in order to achieve your goal. As mentioned earlier, if what you're doing doesn't work, try a different way.

I'll Get to It Later

There is an obvious opposite to perseverance. If perseverance is the continuous pursuit of something, then *procrastination* is the act of delaying taking any action.

Perseverance requires commitment and discipline. Discipline is essentially knowing you need to take action on something and then consciously taking that action. However procrastination occurs when you know you need to take some form of action but allow valuable time to go by before you do anything about it.

Even though many people see procrastination as doing nothing about something, the fact is that a procrastinator is, in fact, doing something. Procrastination is quite simply the act of not acting, of putting things off. It may be as simple as making a decision not to make a decision. In any case, *procrastination is the act of not acting on something.*

So What Causes Procrastination?

Putting things off until later is usually caused by one of two things. The first would be that the required action lacks importance compared to other actions that need to be taken, but that's really more a case of prioritization than it is procrastination. There is nothing wrong with putting something off if there are other more important things that need to be accomplished first.

The major cause of procrastination is something we've already talked about, namely fear. It could be the fear of failing or the fear of success. In either case we sometimes procrastinate so we don't have to face the final outcome. Getting that fear under control, or at least understanding it is there, will help you move toward something on which you might otherwise consider procrastinating. Being aware that you are procrastinating, and of the reasons why you are doing so, will help you make a conscious decision as to whether the thing you are putting off is important enough to pursue with perseverance.

The next time you consider procrastinating about something, ask yourself these questions:

- What will happen if I do nothing?
- What will happen if I do take action?
- Will the penalty for doing nothing be greater or less than the penalty for acting?
- Is there some outcome I am afraid of?
- Is there something more important I should be doing that is causing me not to do this thing?

By answering these questions, you will bring into your awareness exactly why you are considering procrastinating. With this clearer understanding you can make an educated decision as to whether the procrastination is due to other more important priorities or due to plain fear. Once you understand why you are procrastinating, you can consciously decide what to do about it.

Perseverance and the Law of Odds

The law of odds says that, all else being equal, the more times you try something, the greater chance you have of achieving it at least once.

If you pull a card out of a regular deck of playing cards, you have a 1-in-52 chance that a certain card will be drawn. Let's say your card is the queen of diamonds. If you pull a card out and set it aside and it isn't the queen of diamonds, you now have a 1-in-51 chance that the next card will be the one you want. After 5 unsuccessful picks the odds improve to 1-in-47 that the next card will be the diamond queen. With each card pulled, your odds get better. It may take you 52 attempts, but you will eventually pull the queen of diamonds.

The way many people think is that after two or three "pulls" at something, if their "card" hasn't come up, they just give up trying. They don't understand that the more you try at something, the better chance you have of succeeding. Take a good salesperson for example.

The best professional salespeople know this concept well while not-so-successful salespeople don't understand the concept of perseverance as well as they should.

Findings from the National Sales Executives Association demonstrate the importance of perseverance and persistence. These facts can just as easily apply to any other profession or area of life.

- ◆ 80% of all new sales are made after the fifth contact with the same potential customer.

Meanwhile:

- ◆ 48% of all salespeople make one contact with a prospect and then never call on them again.
- ◆ 25% quit after the second call.
- ◆ 12% call three times then quit.
- ◆ Only 10% keep calling until they succeed.

Was the last group of salespeople any more intelligent? Were they better looking? Funnier? Happier? Of course not.

The one thing that was different about the last group of successful salespeople from the less successful ones is that the last 10% of salespeople, those who call on a prospect until they succeed, make up 80% of all sales. This 10% of the sales people get 80% of the business. The only difference between them and the other 90% of salespeople is that *they keep trying while others quit.*

The bottom line is that the more you try to accomplish something, the better chance you have to succeed. Life is a numbers game, and like it or not, you are a player. So remember that you need to succeed only the last time. Just make sure that the first time you try something worthwhile isn't necessarily the *last* time.

Please go to page 181 in your *Making Connections: Plug-It-In and Work-It-Out Tool Kit* and you'll find a tool that can help you persevere at the things important to you. It's called the "Perseverance and Commitment Enhancer." I think you'll find it a helpful tool for ensuring you do follow through on your most important goals. Of course you can find the same tool by logging on to www.EveryAdvantage.net.

Review

1. Perseverance is the steadfast adherence to a course of action, belief, or purpose.
2. Any "wall" will fall if it is beaten on long enough. In the same way, perseverance is the consistent hammering away at something until it finally relents to the effort.
3. The results you want will not always come immediately.
4. One of the key indicators that someone will be successful in life is his or her level of perseverance and persistence in pursuing goals.
5. We often sell ourselves short by quitting either far before, or sometimes even right before, a breakthrough in our progress occurs.
6. One fundamental difference between high achievers and lower achievers is that high achievers will continue to pursue a worthwhile objective even after others would give up trying.
7. Perseverance is not so much what you do or how you do it. Rather it is simply that you do keep trying for the desired result.
8. Procrastination is the act of not acting on something.

9. Perseverance is more likely to occur when one understands that it is a critical factor to success, and that it sometimes takes some time and effort to achieve an objective.

The "Software" of Your Life
The Power of Your Personal Values

When you finish this chapter, you'll:

◆ Know how your thoughts control every result you get, or don't get.
◆ Understand why your subconscious thoughts may be hurting you without your even knowing it.
◆ Recognize the importance of understanding your personal values in order to achieve your goals.
◆ Have identified what your dominant personal values are.

Reality Check

Imagine that you go to a party and see someone you think is really attractive. Now suppose, just suppose, you think to yourself, "Someone like that would never, ever want to talk to me."

After thinking that thought, what would you most likely do?

a) Run right over and ask that person out on a date.
b) Sit tight and wait for him or her to come to you because of your personal magnetism.
c) Go over to the bowl of chips and salsa and eat yourself out of misery.
d) Just go about your business and only talk to that person if someone else introduces you.

Yes, that's right; the answer is most likely "d" and possibly "c" if you are really feeling sorry for yourself. It just makes sense that if you believe that someone doesn't want anything to do with you, you'd probably avoid him or her.

Okay, "rewind" and imagine you're at that same party, same situation, and see that same attractive person, but this time you think to yourself "He/she looks really friendly. I think I'll walk over and introduce myself." After thinking that thought, would you be more likely to:

a) Walk over and introduce yourself.
b) Go over to the bowl of chips and salsa and eat yourself *into* misery.
c) Leave the party.
d) Nothing. Just stand there and think, "I wonder what salsa is made from?"

Yep, right again. The answer is "a." No question about it. If you believed that the other person was approachable, you would be more likely to approach him or her.

Now here's the *big* question. *Why* would you be more likely to do something differently in the second scenario from what you'd do in the first? In both scenarios the party is the *same*. You're wearing the *same* clothes. The person you find attractive is exactly the *same*. It's the *same* time of day. In fact everything is exactly the *same*, except for one thing . . . *your thoughts.*

In fact, the only thing that was different in the two situations was what you thought about the situation. In other words the difference was simply what went through your head or the mental picture in your mind.

Believe it or not, this simple example explains how your life works today and how it will work in the future. I mean, how *everything* in your life will work, period. End of story. No argument. No question. No kidding. Here's a fact that will help you get what you want out of life.

What you do in any situation throughout your whole life will be a result of your total thoughts up to that point. Every action you ever take or decide not to take will be preceded by a thought of some kind that influences or dictates what you will do. Our thoughts result from our programming and in turn become our programming.

If you absorb that simple yet critical concept and do something with it, you can literally dictate the direction of your life. In other words, the direction your life will take is always in your hands, or should I say, *in your mind*.

You Are Your Thoughts

It's been said that a person becomes what he or she thinks about, and that's true. I'm obviously not saying that if you think about a giraffe, you'll become a giraffe. What I am saying is that your thoughts are the force that sets the direction you take in life. Your thoughts directly influence everything you do and who you become.

Throughout your life you become the sum total of every thought you've ever had. And every thought you've ever had will influence the thoughts you'll have in the future. So in order to gain better control of your life, you must first learn to be aware of your thinking. Once you do that, you can learn to control your thinking.

Thoughts are, quite literally, a force of nature. They happen naturally. Like nature, thoughts have the power to create and the power to destroy. However, unlike the forces of nature, which human beings can't control, you can control your thoughts. And because you can control your thoughts, and especially how you react to them, *you can control your life.*

You might say that there are other outside forces that impact what you think. That's true. The things your family says and what your friends say, what your teachers say, and what you hear from the media do impact how you think and what you think about. These are external forces that impact you all the time. However, although these outside factors can *influence* your thinking, they cannot *control* your thinking. Read that last sentence again.

Ally or Enemy

In life your ability to control what you think about will become your single greatest "friend" or "enemy" in determining the direction your life takes. Your way of thinking will directly impact who you become and what you do. In fact your thoughts are the most important tool you have to counteract other unproductive or negative influences in your life.

Think about it this way. Suppose you are in a boat sitting out in the water. What forces could influence where the boat goes in the water? You'll probably answer that the forces are the wind, the currents, and the waves, and you'd be right.

These three major outside forces will directly influence which way the boat goes in the water. But here's the hitch. These external forces alone cannot control the direction of the boat if the driver of the boat doesn't allow them to. The boat's engine, rudder, and sail can allow the captain to overpower, or even use, these outside forces to his advantage.

Let's say the boat has a motor. The motor, if strong enough, can directly influence where the boat goes. A strong motor can fight or counteract the wind, current, and waves to propel the boat in the desired direction. And then there's the rudder. The rudder can have a huge impact on steering the boat. Simply turning the rudder in the right way will help ensure that the boat goes in the right direction. However, like the motor, the rudder can't help you if you don't put it to work.

If the boat is a sailboat, proper use of the sails can have a big influence on the boat's direction as well.

Did you know that a sailboat rarely moves in the direction the wind is blowing? The sail uses the wind to push the boat in the direction the captain wants to go, but the boat's direction is not directly determined by the direction of the wind. If you know anything about how a sailboat works, you'll know this to be true.

So why am I telling you this? Because in life you can overcome . . . and even use . . . the external forces that are trying to influence you to get where YOU want to go.

In life there will always be outside forces that will try to steer you in one direction or another. Like the wind, waves, and current, other people and events in your life will try to take you in their own directions.

The cool thing is that you can be aware of these forces and, just like the boat, not necessarily go in the direction they are trying to push you. You have a choice to decide how you think and what you think about. And all of your decisions in life will be influenced by your thoughts, which are influenced by your personal values and beliefs.

"Think" About It

In order to get what you want in life, your way of thinking must support your personal goals. It *has* to.

Can someone become a great athlete if she doesn't enjoy physical activity? Not likely. Is it possible for someone to form true loving relationships if he fears feeling emotionally attached to someone else? Doubtful. Is it likely one can successfully raise a family if she doesn't like children? Not if the family includes children. And what are the odds that somebody would want to become a pop music star if he doesn't like the idea of being famous? I wouldn't take that bet. Would you?

Will anyone pursue *anything* with passion if doing so is in *direct conflict* with how he or she thinks? You know the answer. Of course not.

Obviously it is important that your thoughts, including your personal values and beliefs, support whatever you want to achieve. You can reach levels of great success in life only if your way of thinking enables you to do so.

Awareness of how you think is the first step in being able to control how you think. (You'll be interested to know that wanting to have a greater understanding of one's self was among the most common desires expressed by the teens in my research.)

Self-understanding is like a road map. You need to see the big picture and know where (or in this case *who*) you are in order to get where you want to go. That may sound a little screwy since you may think you already know who you are. But after completing this chapter and the following chapter, you'll gain additional personal insights that will help catapult you to greater heights. You'll have a greater understanding of how you think and will understand why how you think determines how you see life.

This is an important concept. It's pretty easy to get confused about who you are and what your own values and beliefs are. Let's face it. You've got your friends, parents, teachers, other relatives, and a ton of advertisers trying to convince you that their values and beliefs should be yours (remember the astronauts?). With so much input from others is it any wonder that so many people chase "goals" that are not consistent with what they truly want?

It's easy to get confused about what you want in life if you don't have a crystal clear picture of it in your head.

What's the Big Deal?

Most people past their mid-20s or so will tell you they aren't particularly happy with certain parts of their life—things like their personal finances, social life, career choice, family, friends, health, religion, and so on.

Although life is never perfect, you can take control in getting more of the happiness you want.

Look, you can be as happy as you want to be in life, but to achieve a higher level of happiness, you need to *understand yourself.* In other words you need to recognize exactly what it is that will make you happy. Once you understand that, you need to ensure there is consistency between how you really think and feel and whatever goals you decide to pursue. Without that consistency you will always have a feeling of unease or that something is not completely right.

Molding Your Sidewalk

Early in life the human mind is fluid and flexible, just like fresh concrete being poured to make a sidewalk. This enables the mind to absorb and reflect the characteristics of the world around it. Things like language, attitudes, and values are formed very early.

Like the sidewalk, as you grow up, your ideas, attitudes, and beliefs are "molded" and pretty much conform to the environment or space they're poured into, just like the concrete that is poured to make a sidewalk.

As we get older, the "concrete" of our personal attitudes begins to harden.

In other words our thinking gets more and more rigid until it becomes difficult to change its "shape" at all.

At some point, a solid "foundation" of attitudes and beliefs are established, and just like the concrete in the sidewalk, these personal ways of thinking become rock hard and difficult to break or reshape. That's why as people get older and more established in their thinking, it becomes increasingly difficult for them to make changes in their lives. Their mental "concrete" has hardened. Just as the concrete "sets" in the sidewalk, as we get older, we get "set in our ways" and thoughts. I'm sure you've heard the expression.

But here's the important part. If the concrete sets in the right shape or form, it will create a solid path that will be the foundation for getting you to where you want to go. Likewise, if the concrete hardens in the wrong shape or along the wrong path, you will end up with a path that is bumpy, cracked or headed in the wrong direction.

So if you can create the right form, the right shape, and the right direction for the sidewalk before it hardens, you can determine the path to your destiny. You will design your own sidewalk and where it leads you in life. No *ifs, ands,* or *buts* about it. But in order to make sure it leads you in the right direction, you need to know clearly what the right direction is.

Once the concrete hardens, even if you realize that the path is headed in the wrong direction (and many people don't), it can be very difficult to create a new path. That realization is what many people experience later in life. They realize they're on a path they don't want to be on. The good news is you don't have to go through that experience. You're about to learn how to remold your sidewalk now, if needed, before it gets too hard.

The Balancing Act

There are two driving forces that impact how you think about virtually everything. They are your personal values and your personal beliefs. Both have a direct impact on literally every action and choice you make.

When your values and beliefs are combined, the end product is your attitude toward something. I'm sure you'll agree that your attitude about something impacts how you relate to it and what you may, or may not, do about it.

When your actions are aligned, or consistent, with your personal values and beliefs, you generally enjoy a sense of accomplishment and comfort. You feel good about what you are doing, because there isn't a conflict between what you do and how you feel about it. That's because there is harmony, or balance, between your actions and your thoughts/feelings.

> **If you've ever experienced a situation where you feel less than comfortable, it's more than likely because the situation in some way is in conflict with your personal values or beliefs.**

Compare that balance with the feeling you get when you do things out of line, or inconsistent, with your personal values or beliefs. A feeling of emotional conflict or discomfort will usually occur. Sometimes these feelings will be obvious to you, and other times they will be subtle. But if the conflict is there, feelings of unease will be there too because the balance is gone.

In the same way, if your actions support your personal values and beliefs, you'll find them easier and more enjoyable to take, and you'll be more likely to be successful with them. Let's face it. People like doing things that feel right to them and are less comfortable doing things that don't feel right. It's human nature.

So What Exactly Are Personal Values?

Have you ever lied to somebody or cheated on a test and felt uneasy or bad afterward? If the answer to that question is "yes," you felt that way because you acted in violation of your personal values system that says, "Honesty is important."

Do you want to be wealthy? Would you lie, cheat and steal to achieve wealth?

Are your friendships important to you or would you just as soon steal your best friend's boyfriend or girlfriend?

Given a choice, most of the time, would you rather have the opportunity to get a good physical workout or would you rather relax and watch a movie?

Your answer to some of these questions may be quite clear, or you may be saying, "It depends." In any case, what you value the most will always directly influence how you feel and what you do about everything.

A personal value is just what it sounds like. It's something to which you give a certain worth, desirability, or importance. Just as simple stones vary in value (limestone, granite, marble, quartz, opal, ruby, and diamond), your personal values have different levels of importance to you.

Each time you make any kind of decision, your mind will either subconsciously or consciously "check in" with your personal values system to make the right decision. **Your most dominant (strongest) values will always carry the most weight in the decision-making process** and, given a choice, you'll always want to act consistently with your most dominant personal values.

One way to understand what your strongest personal values are is by paying attention to what you do when you are under pressure. When under pressure (i.e., time constraints or needing to make a decision on something very important) and forced to make a decision, your strongest values will most likely surface. That means that your strongest, or most dominant, values will have the greatest influence over the important decisions you make in life.

Decisions, Decisions

Here's an example of how this all works.

Imagine you're at a party and a friend tells you a secret and clearly asks you not to repeat the secret to anyone. You of course promise not to tell anybody. Not a soul.

Later in the evening it occurs to you that another close friend will be emotionally hurt and tremendously embarrassed if you don't share the secret with her. What would you do?

Would you maintain your integrity with the first friend and keep the secret, or do you honor your loyalty to the other friend and tell her what she probably needs to know? This dilemma is an example of what's known as a "values conflict," and it happens all the time.

Integrity and loyalty are examples of personal values. One person might have a personal values system that says integrity is more important than loyalty and decide to keep the secret. On the other hand someone else might value the concept of loyalty more than integrity and decide to share the secret. The difference in importance of the values to the person may be very small, but one will always be stronger.

In either case, a choice will be made.

Young adults struggle with values decisions like these every day:

◆ My best friend is dating someone I really like. Do I flirt with that person and risk losing my friend?

◆ Do I lie to my parents to get what I want, or do I tell the truth and risk not getting it?

◆ Should I try to "fit in" and do drugs with some other people, or should I stick to my conviction that doing drugs is not smart and maintain my integrity?

◆ When I borrow the family car, should I dangerously race around the city for the sake of fun, or should I stay safe and respect my welfare and that of my passengers?

◆ The music store I work in has a new CD I want, but I don't have the money to buy it. Should I just take it and hope nobody notices?

◆ You're given the opportunity to go on an exciting trip for a month. It sounds like the sort of thing you've always wanted to do. The only problem is that you won't see your boyfriend or girlfriend for a month, and you're not sure you want to do that.

So how would you decide what to do? The same way everybody else does. You would make a decision, consciously or subconsciously, that is most *supportive of your personal values system.*

> **"Your dominant values will have the greatest influence over the decisions you make in life."**

Each of your personal values is like a magnet, and each has a certain degree of strength. All else being equal, the strongest magnet (value) will always draw you to it whenever you have a decision to make. That's why knowing and understanding your personal values system will help you *consciously* make decisions you can feel more comfortable with. If you can consciously understand your values and their importance, making the right decisions will be a lot easier.

Your personal values system determines, to a high degree, who you are as a person. Likewise, your values will always influence the decisions you make in life, so by understanding your personal values system, you can make better decisions.

I'm sure that at one time or another you've experienced an emotional conflict when trying to make an important decision. Maybe it was about whether to hang out with a new and exciting friend rather than an old dependable one. Or maybe the conflict was whether you should study for an important test the next day instead of going to a great concert you were just offered free tickets to.

In either case, maybe you weren't quite sure which decision was best for you. Both options had their positives and negatives. Both had "polarity," meaning that each option had an attraction to you while each also had some degree of repelling force.

Using the "magnet" analogy, have you ever had a feeling of discomfort when you had to make a difficult decision? When that happens, you are wrestling between two or more values of similar strength, with similar "pull," and sometimes you may not even realize it. That can make making the right decision tough.

Here are some more common values decisions you may eventually have to make:

◆ Do I work longer hours to advance my career or should I spend that time with my friends and family?
◆ Should I stay with the security of the job I have but don't really like, or should I pursue another opportunity I'd enjoy where there may be some risk?
◆ Should I spend less time on my favorite hobby to give more of my time to community service?
◆ Should I get more exercise in order to stay healthy, or should I take that time to relax and "veg" out?
◆ Should I run for a leadership position in my club knowing it will take up a lot of time, or should I be just a plain member and free up more of my time?

Many values stay relatively constant over time, although some do change. However, as I mentioned earlier, you'll always be able to recognize what your dominant values are at any given time because, when forced to choose, you'll always pick your most dominant value when under pressure. Let me illustrate.

Let's say you are in your apartment and have your favorite collection of music nicely stored up on the shelves. You've collected the music for several years and are really attached to it.

All of a sudden you smell smoke and hear a neighbor out on the balcony next to yours yelling that he thinks the building is on fire. What would you do?

> **Every decision you will ever make will be affected by your personal values system.**

Would you start to pack up your important belongings and the music collection and try to get them out of the building (risk-taking or nostalgia values) or would you simply bail and say, "Forget the stuff. I am out of here" (safety or security values)?

Whatever the case may be, the tension of the situation will ultimately force your dominant value(s) to the surface, and your dominant value(s) will consciously or subconsciously determine what you do about the situation. In other words you will always be drawn to acting in harmony with the value that has the most strength in that situation.

Most decisions you make will not deal with a situation as intense as the one just described. However, it is the very intensity of each situation that enables you to truly evaluate, understand, and act on your personal values, because the tension causes your strongest values to bubble up.

Here's why this stuff is so important. Throughout life you'll have to make thousands, if not millions, of personal decisions. Decisions about your career, your health, your love life, your money, and so on. Unless your decisions are consistent with your personal values system, you won't feel fulfilled by them, and deep down inside you won't feel right about them. That's why you need to clearly understand your personal values at any point in your life (values can change over time). That understanding will make the difference in helping you make the right decision more often, and making the right decisions can ultimately make you a happier person.

The Values-Goals Connection

When we get to the chapter on personal goal setting, you'll discover just how important it is to have a clear understanding of your personal values. The personal values you already have, and the ones you will continue to develop, will influence how you evaluate virtually every opportunity, alternative, and option in your life. Your values are the underlying force that influences your behavior and thinking at all times.

Your values will determine what you do and how you do it. For that reason *your goals must be in line with your personal values*. If your goals and values aren't lined up consistently with each other, you will feel unfulfilled by achieving your goals. That is, if you do achieve them at all. This situation is very common. Many people try to pursue goals that are not consistent with their own values, because they intellectually "think" the goal is right for them.

For example, let's say a goal of yours is to spend a lot of time with your friends, but you also have a more important goal (based on your values) to feel financially independent. If you end up spending too much time with your buds and sacrifice your ability to gain financial independence, there will always be a little something bothering you in the back of your mind.

> 66 **Unless your goals and decisions are consistent with your personal values, system you won't feel fulfilled by them, and deep down inside you won't feel right about them either.** 99

Values Are Personal

Your values are yours and nobody else's. However, too many people go through life trying to live up to the values of other people including their parents, friends, or other influences. That can happen when one hasn't clearly identified one's own values, so his or her self-concept (an understanding of who he or she is and what he or she wants) is not clear. So these people end up living according to the values of others which at least gives them some sense of direction, even if it's not the right one for them. Unfortunately these values "followers" often don't recognize a personal values conflict until it is too late.

When I was a child my parents didn't have a lot of money. Consequently much of their emphasis to me and my siblings was to pursue a career that offered financial stability. "Be a doctor or a lawyer," I often heard them say.

Being young and naïve, I entered college adopting my parents' values of financial safety and security. They weren't my values, mind you, but my parents had so deeply engrained them in my head that I adopted their values as my own.

It wasn't until many years later that I realized that, although financial stability is an important thing, personal happiness and a love for what I do are even more important to me. It was at that point in life that I started working at what I love.

My goal here is to help you identify your personal values now so that you can determine whether your actions and goals support your values. If it appears that they don't, you will now have a conscious opportunity to take other actions that are in line with your most important values. Doing so will help ensure you a much happier and more satisfying life.

There's No Time Like Right Now

As a young adult you're probably going through a confusing time in life. There are lots of things to consider and important decisions to make. So if you can clarify any amount of this confusion now, you'll have a greater understanding about your life and a better sense of direction and purpose.

One of the things I hear all the time from younger people is that they would like help in determining what they should do with their lives. The reason they want help in this area is that their personal values are often closely intertwined with the values others have laid on them. They don't necessarily consciously realize this, but that is the case.

Deep down inside they still have their own personal values there. They just need a little help in sorting them out from the values that aren't really theirs. Once this is accomplished, understanding one's direction and purpose in life becomes much easier.

Here's the bottom line. You can't live your life with any sense of control unless you have a *plan* for it. You can't plan for your life unless you have personal goals to shoot for. You won't have real *goals* unless you have a conscious purpose, and you can't have a *conscious purpose* unless you realize your underlying personal values and know who you are and what you want for yourself, now and in the future.

Who Are You?

It's not so important to decide early in life *what* you want to be. That will come with greater understanding of your values. The more important thing is to decide now *who* you want to be and how you want to live. Answers to those questions will give you direction and insight into what you want to become and what you want to have.

Many people make the mistake of assuming that "what" they are in life determines "who" they are. They think that who they are is made up of what they do with their life and what they have or own. These "material" things can really influence people, because they associate their status and belongings with their self-worth.

So someone may decide that becoming a doctor, lawyer, politician, archaeologist, or entertainer will determine who they are. Or they may think that owning a BMW® or Lexus® makes them more of a person than driving a Ford® or Suzuki®. These thoughts are a fallacy. Here's why.

Who you are as a person will always be who you are unless you change your personal values and beliefs. You are the sum total of your personal values and beliefs at any given time. That's why what you do with your life, or what you own, does not change who you are. Those factors simply determine what you do and have. Instead who you are will best determine what you should do.

If you depend on your Mercedes-Benz®, Rolex® watch, fame, or a fancy title to determine who you are as a person, you will be sorely disappointed if those things go away.

If you structure your life based on what you have and those material things never appear, you will think less of yourself as a person. And if you do generate some material things or status that later disappear from your life, then who you think you are disappears as well. But who you are can never actually disappear. Hang in with me here. This is an important concept to get.

Who You Are/Your Self-Worth

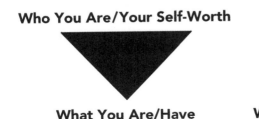

What You Are/Have

What You Are/Have

Who You Are/Your Self-Worth

Look at the illustrations on the previous page. Assuming these were real objects, which of the two triangles appears less likely to be knocked over, the one sitting on a tiny point or the one sitting on a sturdy base? Of course, the triangle sitting on the sturdy base would be seen as more stable. It would be easy to "tip over" the triangle on the left, but difficult to make the one on the right lose balance.

To compare this to life, like it or not, who you are is the constant, the foundation, the baseline, the thing that will always be there. Your whole life will be a reflection of who you are. And nobody can take away from you who you are as a person. It can't be done. You are who you are.

What can be taken from you is what you are or what you have. What you are and have are external factors; who you are is an internal condition. So why is it that so many people decide that what they are, or what they have, determines who they are? Why is that?

Here's the inside scoop on this little paradox. Those who believe that what they have determines who they are have made a decision. They have decided they are less of a person without what they have or think they should have. That way of thinking is part of who they are. That's why they depend on having things or status to fill up their need to feel important.

Now I'm not saying that having nice things or having status are not good things. They are good things as long as having them is a result of who you are and that you do not use them to determine who you are, because, again, who you are is who you are.

Who you are as a person will determine what you want to have, but what you have does not determine who you are.

In a moment we're going to work on helping you understand your personal values. Your values are the things that genuinely determine who you are as a person. And once you understand who you are and what you're all about, you'll find it a whole lot easier determining what you should be, what you should do and should have, making those things consistent with who you are.

Understanding Your Personal Values

We're ready to begin our active journey of self-understanding. This is a critical exercise that will impact your whole life by bringing you a greater understanding of yourself.

Remember:

> You cannot achieve what you want in life if you don't understand what you value, because if you don't understand what you value, you really don't know what you want to achieve.

Please go to page 183 in your *Making Connections: Plug-It-In and Work-It-Out Tool Kit* or log onto www.EveryAdvantage.net to find and complete an exercise called "My Personal Values."

Is Doing the Right Things a Value of Yours?

Congratulations on completing this important exercise on self-understanding. Remember, I promised not to give you any advice I could be wrong about, so if you skipped doing the personal values exercise, please do it now! Understanding your personal values is a critical step that will help you better understand your life. If you completed the exercise, I congratulate you on your wisdom. In the next chapter you'll learn about how your personal belief system affects your life.

Review

1. Without exception, how you think about things, and what things you think about, will dictate the actions you take and the results you get. If you want to get different results from those you are currently getting, you must change your way of thinking.
2. Your thoughts are your software, and they dictate what you will and won't do throughout life.
3. Your thoughts are cumulative. Every thought you ever have will in some way influence your future way of thinking.
4. Being aware of what you are thinking is a critical first step

to self-understanding.

5. Molding your concrete now, before it hardens, will be a lot easier to do than to try to change what is "set" in the future.

6. Your personal values will substantially influence what you do and how you feel about what you do.

7. Every decision you will ever make will be influenced by your personal values system.

8. Your personal goals must be consistent with your values for you to feel fulfilled by achieving them.

9. If you don't clearly understand what you value, then you really don't understand who you are or what you want.

The "Software" of Your Life
The Impact of Your Personal Beliefs

When you finish this chapter, you'll:

- See how your beliefs affect what you do or don't do.
- Know why your beliefs aren't necessarily true.
- Know how to create the right kinds of beliefs to empower you.
- Understand which of your personal beliefs may be holding you back from achieving all you can.

Personal Beliefs

Now that you've developed a better understanding of your personal values, let's look at your personal belief system. *A personal belief is your opinion, position, sentiment, or view about something.* Beliefs are what you think is true.

Your beliefs, like your values, are based on your past experiences. They are formulated over time and are influenced by your senses. Experiences that affect your beliefs include what you see, hear, smell, taste, feel, or otherwise sense.

Like personal values, personal beliefs are often affected by the opinions of others, and people frequently adopt the beliefs of others as their own.

So a belief is a personal truth. It is the way you "see" things, and the way you see things determines how you act on, or react in, any given situation.

 Although beliefs are the way we see the world, our beliefs aren't necessarily always the way things *really* are. They aren't always the truth. Let's look at a few examples that illustrate this.

Way to Go, Chris!

In the 1400s the common belief was that the world is flat. That was the "truth" at the time. People were convinced that the world was flat, because they saw the horizon and determined there had to be a point at which they would fall off the earth if they kept heading in that direction.

This belief was based on something they saw (remember, beliefs are formulated through your senses), and enough people agreed with the concept of a flat world that their opinions influenced those of many others. It was a mass illusion based on their imagination. Nonetheless it was a strong belief and therefore was "real" to those who believed it. If you were alive at that time in history, chances are you also would have believed that the world is flat.

In 1492 Christopher Columbus changed this belief for everyone, forever. The fact was that the world was never flat although most people believed it was. Fortunately there were a few people who believed something different, and they were willing to risk an ocean voyage with Columbus to confirm their belief. The sailors who believed the world might be round instead of flat saw the potential for a different truth. In doing so, they changed the course of the world from that point on. The firm belief that the world was flat was changed forever.

Here's the point. Nothing about the earth actually changed. The world was always as it was, round. Only the belief that the earth was flat changed, and this one change in belief completely altered human history. It changed what people did and how they perceived the world. One erroneous belief, proved wrong, completely changed the future of civilization.

Are there beliefs you might have that, if changed, would alter the way you look at things or change what actions you would or would not take? I'll bet there are.

I Want to Believe Like Mike

Did you know that Michael Jordan couldn't make his high school basketball team the first time he tried out for the Junior Varsity squad? The coach obviously believed that Jordan didn't have the talent or potential to play basketball. Makes you laugh now, doesn't it?

Jordan didn't make the team cut because of what the coach believed, not because of what Jordan believed or because of what was actually true. Perhaps Jordan wasn't as good a player in high school as he became in college or in the NBA, but the potential was always there. There's no arguing the point. What is just is!

The good news is that there was someone who believed that Michael Jordan could play basketball. That person was Michael Jordan.

Would Jordan have ever made his high school basketball team, not to mention the NBA, if he agreed with the initial beliefs of the high school coaches? Of course not. He would have stopped trying to play basketball (sounds like beliefs impact perseverance). But he didn't believe his coach's opinion of him. He had his own empowering beliefs, and the rest is history.

Think about this for a second. If Jordan decided to believe his high school basketball coach's initial opinion of him, he would probably have given up playing the game even though his potential and abilities would have been identical in every way. Only his belief would have stopped him. Fortunately that wasn't his belief, and he didn't give up on himself.

> 66 **The fact was that the world was never flat although most people believed it was.** 99

Slow Down—You're Doing the Impossible

Until 1954 nobody had ever run a timed mile in under four minutes. In fact a sub-four-minute mile was believed to be humanly impossible, unattainable.

Then came along a British athlete named Roger Bannister. Bannister believed he could break the four-minute barrier in running a mile, and on May 6, 1954, Roger Bannister ran a mile in 3 minutes 59.4 seconds at Oxford, England. His historic run permanently changed everyone's belief that a sub-four-minute mile was possible. A new paradigm was born.

But there's an even more amazing twist to this story. Within one month of Bannister's historic run, Australian runner John Landy broke Bannister's record, and more than 25 people have since broken the four-minute barrier more than 65 times.

Once the belief that nobody could humanly run a sub-four-minute mile changed, the barrier was gone. But was there ever really a barrier except for the belief itself?

The fact is that there was no four-minute barrier except a mental one, an inaccurate belief. The belief itself was holding people back from achieving their true potential until Bannister proved the belief wasn't a fact. That's because it was not his belief. It was not how he saw the truth.

At one time mankind believed the "truth" that human beings can't fly, that is until the Wright brothers saw a different truth and the airplane was invented.

It was once believed impossible for a human to breathe under water without a lifeline and a deep sea diving uniform. Then along came a sea adventurer named Jacques Cousteau who saw a different truth. Cousteau created a new device called the "aqua lung," and SCUBA (Self-Contained Underwater Breathing Apparatus) diving became possible.

 All of the above examples illustrate the power of beliefs and that, once a belief is changed, a new reality emerges. In other words, **a belief isn't necessarily the truth. It is only a perceived truth.**

So let's get back to you. Are all of your beliefs the indisputable facts? That's a very important question to answer, since your beliefs will impact all of your opinions, decisions, and actions regarding what is possible for the rest of your life—that is, unless you change them.

Burn this thought into your brain. **What you believe, whether that belief is fact or fiction, determines what you do and how you react to virtually everything.** *Everything.* **But** *everything* **you believe isn't necessarily true.**

If you have beliefs that hold you back in life, you need to identify those beliefs now and challenge them to see if they are actual facts. (Chances are they are not.)

If you believe that your incorrect beliefs are facts, you will find them difficult to overcome. On the other hand if you are willing to accept that some of your beliefs may not be the whole truth, you will be open to examining them more closely. Therein lies the key.

Types of Beliefs

There are essentially two categories of beliefs. The first is an "empowering belief," or a belief that can help you achieve your goals. These are also known as "constructive beliefs."

If a belief reflects optimism, progress, and confidence, then it will help you. The belief will support your ability to achieve the goals and dreams you seek. Examples of empowering beliefs might include:

- ◆ I am loveable.
- ◆ People like me for who I am.
- ◆ My health is very important.
- ◆ My faith supports me each day.
- ◆ I am smart.
- ◆ Others find me a fun and attractive person.
- ◆ I am destined to be successful.
- ◆ I'm not perfect, and that's okay.
- ◆ I can do whatever I put my mind to.

Each of these beliefs would help someone take actions that a person with more negative beliefs might not.

What would your life be like if you had only constructive beliefs? If you really had deep beliefs like the examples above, what would you be likely to do? How would you act? Would you do anything differently than you do now? Would your life show more promise if you had such beliefs?

The second type of belief is a "limiting belief." Limiting beliefs are those that will stifle your ability to achieve your goals. These beliefs can also be referred to as "destructive beliefs."

If a belief reflects doubt, fear, defeatism, or negativity, it is a limiting belief and it can only work against you. A limiting belief will lead you to become less of a person, not more. Examples of limiting beliefs might include:

◆ Everyone else is better than me.
◆ What I have determines who I am.
◆ I'll never be a happy person.
◆ I am not smart enough.
◆ I have no potential as a student.
◆ I am destined to be a failure.
◆ I can't accomplish anything.
◆ Others don't find me attractive.
◆ I don't deserve to be successful.

What would your life be like if you had only destructive beliefs? If deep down inside you were full of beliefs like these examples, what would you be more likely to do or not do? How might these kinds of beliefs change the way you act? How might they affect what you accomplish in life?

Beliefs like these will limit what you do and how you see the world. The good news is that you can change your self-limiting beliefs into empowering ones.

Now that we understand the impact beliefs can have, it's time to take a closer look at your own beliefs.

Please go to page 195 in your *Making Connections: Plug-It-In and Work-It-Out Tool Kit* or log onto www.EveryAdvantage.net and find the exercise called "My Personal Beliefs." When you finish, we'll come back here and talk about how you can make your beliefs work for you.

Believe It or Not!

Let's continue now and learn some more valuable insights to help you better understand and manage your beliefs to your advantage.

Now that you've completed the exercise on beliefs (I'm assuming you did!), one of my objectives is to convince you that chances are that most, if not all, of your destructive beliefs are not an absolute fact. In a moment I'll show you a way you can actually experience your limiting beliefs as not true.

Let's take another look at how one's beliefs can dramatically change his or her actions in the following story.

You Won the Sweepstakes!

There's a story of a saleswoman who traveled to Chicago to sell a new account—a very large and important account. She needed to make this particular sale to reach her sales goal for the year and earn her bonus, but she wasn't feeling very confident that she would be successful. In fact she believed that the potential customer would turn her down, because it had happened so many times before with that person.

The salesperson had a lot at stake with this sales call and desperately needed to make the sale and receive her bonus money.

The morning she woke up to make the sale, she was very nervous. Very, very nervous.

As she was walking out of her hotel room to make the sales call, the phone rang. The saleswoman picked it up and heard a loud voice on the other end of the line. It was her husband, and he seemed very, very happy.

"Honey, are you sitting down?" her husband said excitedly. "You'll never believe what happened. Friendly Publishers left us a voice mail saying that we've won! We won the sweepstakes!! You don't have to work in that high-pressure job anymore. You can now do something with your life that you really want."

"How much did we win?" she asked curiously.

"I'm not sure," he replied. "I haven't been able to reach them. I'd think that they would call you only if you win a big prize. It's got to be at least a million dollars."

The woman was shocked for a moment and then thrilled. In a split second she realized that her life had just changed dramatically "What should I do now?" she thought. "I don't need to make this dumb sales call. Oh, what the heck," she decided. "I'm here already. I'll go ahead and make the sales call anyway. It'll be fun. I'll give it my best shot, but if the customer turns me down again, no big deal."

The saleswoman proceeded to the prospect's office with a great sense of personal security and confidence. She knew she didn't have to make the sale, so all the pressure was gone.

An hour and a half later the saleswoman walked out of the prospect's office with a signed contract. It was her biggest sale ever. "Could this day be going any better?" she thought.

When she got back to her hotel room, the saleswoman noticed that the message light on her phone was blinking. She called the front desk and learned that her husband had tried to reach her, so she called him back immediately.

"Honey," he said, "I don't know how to tell you this. After I spoke with you, Friendly Publishers called again. It turns out we did win a nice prize, but it was only a wide-screen TV set. We didn't win the big cash prize."

Okay, here's the question. Was the saleswoman's financial condition really any different before she made the sales call than it was afterward? Was she really "rich" at any time? Of course she wasn't, but her belief that she was now financially secure completely changed the way she acted on the sales call and had a dramatic impact on her level of self-confidence.

Her belief that she won at least one million dollars was never a fact, but it was real to her at the time. The saleswoman really believed that she was now financially secure, and that belief alone was enough to give the woman the confidence needed to make the sale.

This story illustrates how our beliefs, whether they are good or bad, can have a dramatic influence on what we do. In this case the saleswoman's belief that she was now financially independent and didn't have to worry about whether she made the sale or not affected her approach to the customer. Her sense of confidence translated into a more effective sales call, and she made the sale.

All of this happened when, in fact, nothing had actually changed in the woman's life other than her belief that she was no longer desperate for the money. The pressure was removed, simply by a changed belief.

I have to tell you that sometimes I blame my wife or kids because they move my keys or glasses to somewhere other than where I put them. The kicker is that most of the time it turns out that I was the bozo who moved them or didn't remember where I'd actually left them. So I blame them for what I believe to be true, but the truth is often not a fact.

Have you ever had an experience like that? If you're like most people, you have.

Perception Is Reality

Right now, you may think your destructive, limiting beliefs are true. That's because you're looking at them through what's known as a "perceptional filter." That means you see something in a certain way because you have only a limited amount of information to evaluate it. We say the information is "filtered" since you see things only from your current perspective or reality. Your mind allows only certain information to filter through, and this limited information supports or makes up your beliefs. That means that sometimes your beliefs are based on an illusion, a mistaken perception of reality. In fact it happens more often than you may think.

Take a look at the picture to the right. You probably believe that these people had significant influence in the world.

Now take a look at the picture again. When you first looked at it, chances are you believed it was former President Bill Clinton and his vice-president, Al Gore, for at least a moment, right? In fact, it's actually Clinton's face with two different haircuts.

You probably saw the photo as Clinton and Gore because you expected to and because of the way I introduced the picture (e.g., "You probably believe that these people had significant influence in the world"). You were already led to believe that the people were Clinton and Gore, because you filtered the available information based on the bogus information I offered you. In a sense you believed what you wanted to believe, because I handed you some information that made you do so. It was easier for your mind to accept it than it was to examine it.

You didn't really take in all there was to see, and our personal belief systems are often developed in the same way. Here's another example.

What Happened?

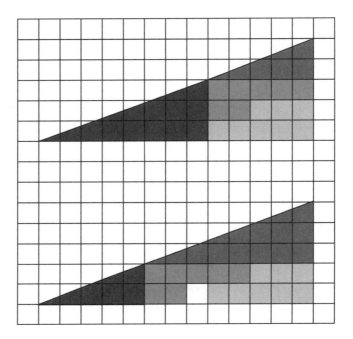

In the top figure in the graphic above, you can see what the puzzle looks like before the parts are moved around. In the bottom figure the parts are moved around and the total figure is the same size, right? So where does the "hole" come from in the bottom figure?

You can find the answer if you look just a little closer. The top figure appears to be a triangle, but it isn't. This figure actually has four sides, two of which are what appear to be the diagonal "straight line" at the top. In fact the top surface of the figure is two lines that come together at a *very* slight angle. Look at how the corresponding squares compare along the diagonal "line" in both figures and you'll see what I mean.

It is the slight "curve" in what appears to be the top line that makes the figure take up slightly less space than if it were a true triangle—the exact amount of space, as a matter of fact, as the empty block in the bottom figure takes up. It's an illusion that the two figures appear to be the same shape, but they do both take up exactly the same amount of space.

Here's one more example. At first glance do the horizontal lines in the drawing above look parallel or do they look slanted?

The fact is they are parallel. However, if you were to look at the drawing quickly without really studying it, your mind would tell you (believe) that the lines are slanted. Not until you really study the drawing can you filter out the information that throws you off. Although first impressions often form our beliefs, first impressions don't always tell the whole story.

The way we see the world sometimes works like the filter on a coffee maker. The filter lets only the water and tiny particles of coffee flavor through, which means that only a limited essence of the actual coffee beans ever makes it through to the coffee pot. The whole of the coffee beans never makes it through, so, in a sense, a large part of the full "truth" of the coffee is filtered out.

When you drink coffee, you are drinking only a small fraction of the coffee beans used to make it, so you are not fully experiencing the coffee. Instead you taste only the water and a small trace of the beans that makes it through the filter to give it flavor.

But what would happen if you removed the filter? The coffee would undoubtedly taste and feel different in your mouth. It would be a different experience than drinking the filtered coffee, a different reality. Not necessarily a better or worse experience, just a different one. It would be a different "truth."

In the case of the photo of President Clinton, I helped you decide what information to filter as well as what information you needed to take in.

Once you see the whole truth, however, your belief about what something is or isn't may be completely different. That's partly why I started this book with the subject of awareness. Awareness is very important.

Life works in the same way. All our beliefs are based on only the information that makes it through our perceptional filter, only what we are aware of. **Our beliefs are based only on the information we take in, but that doesn't necessarily make them true.**

Remember, a belief is a perceived truth and may or may not be a fact. For instance if you are broke and don't have any money, to have the belief, "I'm broke," would not be a destructive belief. That would be a fact . . . the real truth. The belief in this case would be true.

Instead a destructive belief in this instance might be, "I'll never have any money" since this is a possible belief but not necessarily a fact. It can't be proven and is based only on what you perceive, so it is only a belief and not a fact. The reason this belief would be destructive is that if you actually believe you will never have any money, your actions will become consistent with your beliefs and almost ensure that your belief comes true. The mind does not like to be proven wrong.

Act As If

Go back to the "My Personal Beliefs" exercise you did and look at the list of 5 destructive beliefs you recorded earlier. After you review your list of 5 personal destructive, limiting beliefs, I want you to pick one of the beliefs for an experiment. This is called the "Act As If" experiment. Here's the way it works.

First you choose a limiting belief you want to change and, for the next three days, act as if the opposite of the belief is true. You may need to psych yourself up to do this, but it will be worth it. Make a game of it and have some fun.

While you play this little game, you shouldn't let anyone else know you are doing it. That will only make the exercise more difficult for you. It will also prevent you from getting a true reading on how well this exercise can work for you.

Let's say the limiting belief you are working on is, "I'm never any fun. People think I'm boring." For the next three days your job is to convince yourself that you are fun and that people find you very interesting, so just act as if that were true. Be confident about it. Don't be concerned with other peoples' reaction to you. Just play the part like you're in a movie. If other people don't give you the reaction you want or expect, assume they are having a bad day, not you. (In fact this is often the case anyway when others don't act as we wish they would.)

When you adopt the more productive belief, you are literally changing the filter through which you are seeing your experiences. And when you change the filter, the experience changes as well.

What you should notice during the three days you "Act As If" is that you will actually recognize points in the day where *your limiting belief no longer seems true,* because your new "filter" is looking to be proven right. It may not happen all the time at first, but you'll notice that you will find specific instances where your belief is false. And if you can find exceptions to your limiting belief, then your limiting belief is obviously not true.

You may ask, "How will I all of a sudden start to see exceptions to my limiting belief?"

The answer is because your subconscious will begin looking for exceptions to support your new belief rather than looking for evidence to support the limiting belief. Remember, your mind will search for what you ask it to.

In the example we used, your mind would be looking for reactions from other people to support your new belief that you are fun as opposed to always expecting others to find you dull.

In the example of a limiting belief we just used, if you look for opportunities to prove that you are dull, you will find them. Likewise if you look for signs that prove you are not dull, you will find them too.

Once you notice instances where your new belief is supported, you will recognize that the belief you thought was totally true has some flaws in it. And if the belief has flaws in it, the belief is *not a fact.*

If you play the "Act As If" game long enough, you will see one of two things begin to happen. First you might see that your original limiting belief was not well founded in the first place (most aren't) and that it was just in your head. Your mind will note that the belief isn't a universal fact, and since you now know it isn't a fact, you'd no longer hold it as your belief.

Secondly you may find that you actually changed your behavior (a behavior you'll want to stick with) to make the limiting belief untrue. Therefore the limiting belief is no longer yours since you know it doesn't have to be the way you formerly saw it.

Do this exercise with as many destructive beliefs as you'd like and feel free to use your *FlashPoints* Log to record your observations. Once you start consciously changing your perception of things and looking for the exceptions to your limiting beliefs, you'll find that everything starts to look more positive to you. And when things look better, you feel better.

By the way, if you are saying to yourself, "That won't ever work for me," you are displaying a form of belief called an *expectation*. An expectation is nothing more than the belief that something will probably happen or not happen. So change your expectation too for the sake of this exercise. Just suspend your limiting belief for three days and see what happens.

Review

1. Your beliefs are how you see things—your personal truth.
2. All your beliefs may seem like facts, but many may not be facts at all because you often form them through a perceptional filter.
3. There are two kinds of beliefs: empowering beliefs and limiting beliefs.
4. You need to test your limiting beliefs to see if they are really facts or simply perceptions.

PART THREE

The "Software" of Your Life
It All Adds Up to Attitudes

When you finish this chapter, you'll:

♦ Understand better what creates your personal attitudes about things.

♦ See clearly why having personal passion for something is so important to your achieving the highest level of success.

♦ Know how to determine your personal passion and purpose.

♦ Have a different perspective on what "work" is supposed to be.

Personal attitude is a critical factor in determining one's ability to achieve something, whether that something is big or small. That said, in this chapter we'll review the impact your attitude has on your entire life.

When you combine your values and your beliefs, you get a by-product called "attitude." Your attitude is your opinion or feeling about something. It's how you see things. Your attitude will have an enormous impact on how you react to anything. In fact, since it consists of two powerful factors, values and beliefs, attitude is the primary influencer of your behavior. If you can control your attitude, you will control your life. Let me repeat that.

Control your attitude and you will control your life.

Three Sides of Success—a.k.a. The Success Triad

There are essentially three things that determine your ability to succeed at *anything*. I call them "The Success Triad." They are:

◆ **Knowledge,** or what you know

◆ **Skills,** or what you can do with what you know

◆ **Attitude**, or how you view things overall based on your values and beliefs

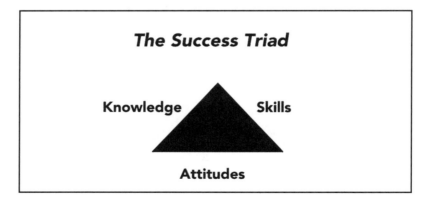

Notice that "attitude" is at the foundation, or base, of the success triad.

Let's use an analogy to illustrate the importance of attitude, which is by far the most critical element of the success triad since it influences the other elements so much.

Let's pretend that your knowledge equals the raw materials you have to work with, like in a factory. Everything you know can be used to produce or create some form of output or outcome.

Your skills are the tools or machines you have to work with in the factory. They allow you to take the knowledge (raw materials) and apply or use it to do something. By the way, just because you have knowledge about something doesn't mean you have the skills needed to use that knowledge.

Finally let's call your attitude toward something the factory building itself, the overall environment. The size of the factory (attitude) dictates the physical capacity to produce the end product.

The larger the factory (in other words, the more "open" the attitude), the more product can be produced in it. That's because the amount of raw materials and tools the factory can hold is directly proportional to the size of the factory. A small factory would hold fewer materials or tools, while a large factory would hold a lot.

If your attitude toward something is that you have little interest (apathy) or your attitude is negative, we'd call that a small, uninviting, and limited factory space. When your capacity (or attitude about something) is low, chances are you wouldn't spend much time trying to develop your ability to do it well, since your "factory" won't make room to "accept" the raw materials (knowledge) and tools (skills) needed to get good at that particular thing.

For instance if your friends ask you to host a party but you aren't interested (negative attitude toward hosting a party) in doing so for whatever reason, you wouldn't care enough to put your full heart and effort into doing a good job at it.

Your attitude determines your willingness or openness to acquire certain knowledge and skills. I'm sure you'll agree that if you have the ability to do something but not the willingness, you'd probably never care enough about it to get really good at it.

You might say that if you have the willingness to do something, but not the ability, you wouldn't get very good at that thing either. That's certainly true. However, if you have little ability to do something but have the willingness to learn more about it or to get better at it, you can, and most likely will, get better at it.

All things being equal, even if you have the ability to do something, you must also have a genuine desire to improve at it or you'll never achieve your best. Keep in mind that your best may not make you "the" best, but it will be your best, and that's what counts.

So, if you have access to the raw knowledge and skills to do something, but don't have an attitude of interest toward it, you will most likely not pursue whatever it is with any kind of passion. Why would anyone pursue getting additional knowledge or developing more skills at something if his interest level in that "something" is low? He wouldn't.

The bottom line is if you don't have the right attitude about something, you can never maximize your potential because you won't care enough about it to do so.

Be Passionate about Passion

I've been asked a lot how one really knows if someone has found his or her passion in life. To answer that question, let's first look at what passion is.

If attitude is how you look at things and how you look at things determines how interested you might be in something, then passion is the ultimate attitude reflecting the level of interest you have in something. A passion is, quite simply, something you feel very strongly about.

The things you are most passionate about will be those things into which you are most willing to invest more time and energy. Your passions make you feel good and fulfilled simply by being involved with them. They are "worth your time." And since it is everyone's goal to feel good in some way or another, your life needs to involve a passion of yours.

Here's why I bring up this subject. According to Charles Templeton, author of *Succeeding—What It Takes,* it's been found that as many as 93% of adults are doing things with their life that they have little or no passion about. They simply wander through life and end up in a place they never wanted or intended to be. It's no surprise that a similar percentage of adults say they are not happy with their jobs.

Earl Nightingale, author of *The Strangest Secret,* reported that in the U.S. only 1 out of 37 people, or just less than 3%, respond that they are in their work because they love what they do. If you compare that number to the percentage of people who have attracted great wealth, you'd discover that the top 3% of people make up most of the wealth in the U.S. Is it a coincidence that about 3% of people really enjoy what they do and that 3% have gathered the most wealth? Is it possible that they are the very same people in most cases? Hmmmm.

Too many people are influenced by parents, friends, peers, teachers, and other relatives to make important decisions about life that draw them away from pursuing their true passions. That's why so many people let life happen to them rather than making their ideal life happen.

University of Chicago Professor Mihaly Csikszentmihalyi (yes, unusual name, but he's a bright guy) explains that one of the biggest problems in society is that we have divided life into two distinct categories. The first is "work," or the things we do that we feel are necessary but unpleasant, and "play," which are the things we enjoy but find basically meaningless.

According to Professor Csikszentmihalyi, studies show that by the sixth grade children have learned to feel unhappy, bored, and weak when they are doing anything they think of as "work" and to feel happy, excited, and strong when they do anything they define as "play."

This creates a challenging situation to overcome in that we are taught at a very young age that work is important for us and that play is not as important. This may sound familiar to you.

With that way of thinking we create a situation where we can never be satisfied. We learn to do either something we see as tedious but necessary ("work") or something we believe to be enjoyable but pointless ("play").

In other words we are "taught" early on in life to believe that we shouldn't enjoy what we consider work. Likewise we learn to believe that anything we enjoy isn't "acceptable" as work. This way of thinking leads a vast majority of people to pursue paths in life that they don't enjoy. Therefore their "work" feels like work.

There is a direct correlation between one's enthusiasm for something (level of passion) and the amount of effort she or he will dedicate to it.

Personal satisfaction and passion are at the top of the list of important ingredients to success. That's because it takes personal satisfaction to become and feel "successful."

> **"Too many people simply let life happen to them rather than making their ideal life happen."**

> **"Since it is everyone's goal to feel good in some way or another, your life needs to involve a passion of yours."**

Think about it. How can you feel successful at something you don't enjoy doing? The fact is you'll always put more effort into, and become more successful at, something you like doing.

Can you name one thing you're as good at as you possibly could be that you don't enjoy doing? The odds are that the answer is "no."

Doing What You Love

Here's a question for you. If you were financially independent, what is the one thing you would do with your time? The answer to this question will reveal your primary passion. Some people think that if they just earn a lot of money, one day they will be able to do what they want to do. On the surface that seems to make sense. But at the same time it's easy to understand that, all else being equal, if you can do what you really love in your life, you'll be more likely to get good at it. Likewise you'll be more likely to get paid more for something you do well. So if you do something you love, it is a win-win situation for you!

If you find a way to integrate your passion into your life, particularly if you can do so in your career, you will increase your chances of success and happiness a thousand-fold. So do what you love to do, and the rest will take care of itself.

 Only you can decide if you are going to do something with your life that you want to do or if you'll do something with your life because others think it's what you "should" be doing.

Please go to page 199 in your *Making Connections: Plug-It-In and Work-It-Out Tool Kit* or log onto www.EveryAdvantage.net and look for the exercise entitled "Determining Your Passion." You'll find it extremely useful in helping you understand better what you love doing. After you've completed the exercise come back here.

Your Passion Will Balance You

You may at this point say to yourself, "Yeah, that's nice, but my passion isn't a practical thing to pursue as a career." If that's the case, ask yourself this question, "Is that me talking or is it simply the opinion of others?"

Think carefully about what you've decided. If your reasons for pursuing your passion are strong enough, you can do it. If your reasons are strong enough, the answers to how to get it done will follow. When you know what you want and what interests you and you want it with passion, you will find ways to achieve it. The answers and solutions will become apparent to you in time.

When you select a direction for your life that involves your passion, your life becomes more balanced and meaningful. It becomes your center of gravity. Everything just feels better . . . where it should be.

If you stand up straight, you are very well balanced, right? You can move easily in any direction you want. You are on your center of gravity, and you can maneuver with ease.

But if you are leaning over on one foot so far that you are away from your center of gravity, pretty soon you will be putting all of your effort into struggling just to stay up and balanced.

Likewise if you choose to do something with your life that allows you to be balanced, something that is at the center of your "gravity," you'll be able to move successfully in the direction you want easily rather than spending all of your time struggling just to stay "standing up."

I encourage you not to think in terms of what is the practical thing to do. In life we often learn to get too practical too soon. When you say you want to do something, your family or friends often say, "What are you doing that for?". . . "What good is that?" . . . "That's not practical!"

Instead go with your passion. Do something with your life that you love. The ultimate attitude of passion will drive you to high levels of achievement if you allow it to.

Review

1. Your values and beliefs combine into what is known as your attitude.
2. Passion is the ultimate attitude of interest and enthusiasm.
3. Work does not have to be "work."
4. Do what you love to do and you will have the needed energy to become great at it. Then whatever rewards you want will follow.

"Program" Yourself for Success
What You Think . . . You Will

When you finish this chapter, you'll:

◆   See how your mind has actually been "programmed" ever since you were very young.
◆   Understand how to gain greater control over
your thoughts and therefore over the results
you get in life.
◆   Have a clearer picture of how you think and
how that currently impacts what you do.
◆   Understand why your personal expectations
can determine pretty much what your life
will look like.

Software for Your Mind

I n this chapter of _FlashPoint_ we're going to explore the similarities between how
your mind works and how a computer works. I think you'll find the compari-
son valuable in helping you understand your own internal "programming."

Let's say you buy a new computer, a top of the line, state-of-the-art system with all the newest fancy features.

Next you select some cool software and take the whole thing home to set it up. An hour or so later you've got the system assembled. You've loaded the software and you start to work (or play).

While checking out a couple of the software programs and cruising the Internet, you notice that there seems to be a "bug" or two in the software because it's not doing what you want it to. Although you try to figure out what the problem is, the software keeps messing up. In order to try to fix the problem, you reboot the system and change some settings thinking that will fix the problem, but it doesn't. After some additional frustration you turn the system off and go to bed figuring it might just be a glitch that you can fix tomorrow.

When you boot up the next day, the problems continue, only they're slightly worse than they were before. Eventually you determine you have a virus on the system, because you realize you were on the Net and hadn't loaded the virus software yet. So you load the software, detect the virus, and eliminate the problem before any more damage is done. You wipe your forehead realizing that if you hadn't fixed the problem, over time that one little virus could have virtually destroyed all of the computing potential the system had.

People are, in many ways, the same as a computer. Your body is the computer "housing" and your brain is the "hard drive" that processes all of the information.

Each of us is born with a natural hard drive that contains complex read-only memory (ROM) that has evolved and upgraded over thousands of years. Your human "ROM" keeps your heart beating, your food digested, your hair growing, and your eyes focused. It determines a lot about your core personality and other bodily functions you have little, if any, control over. This "read-only" software is simply there. It comes with the hardware on the hard drive of your brain. You can't write over it, and in most cases, you don't want to write over it.

"Application" programming is a different story. That's the software that enables you to do certain things. You begin loading application software from the time you are born. However the software that's loaded isn't always up to you.

First your parents start to program you as a baby. They begin to develop your self-esteem and sense of security. They help you learn how to react to things by modeling behavior for you. They influence your eating habits, teaching you about broccoli and Brussels sprouts as well as candy and cake.

Through trial and error you develop some of your own software that eventually teaches you to walk, to talk, and to play.

Later your friends and teachers begin to program and influence you. Your friends help program you to learn what it takes to be liked, accepted, and respected—in other words, what is socially acceptable and what isn't. Your teachers also program you with a lot of data, like math, history, science, and reading, not to mention a bunch of other stuff like good conduct and what type of behavior it takes to earn positive feedback. The media and advertisers program you to establish their definition of success or beauty, and so on.

Much of the application programming we receive early in life occurs without our even realizing it. Then before we know it, we've been programmed how to think, what to focus on, and everything else our mind does. But just like a computer, our programming is not perfect. There may be a few bugs . . . a few flaws . . . in the program that can mess things up.

Worse yet, a lot of people . . . and I mean an awful lot . . . end up with the equivalent of at least one self-sabotaging computer "virus" in their heads—a program, or two, or three that sabotage and undermine the rest of the programming. The result of this virus is that it limits in some way our ability to achieve what we would ideally like to achieve. And to make things even worse we usually don't even know it's happening. Examples might be an unproductive belief or a destructive personal value that operates in the background.

> **"Your input programming comes from a wide range of sources, and as a young child you have little control over what is programmed."**

That little software "bug," gone unchecked, will do damage to your ability to get the most out of life. It will sabotage your best-intended efforts, because it is working in your mind without your even noticing. It's not a scary "sci-fi" thing I'm talking about here. It's simply how the mind works.

There has been a long list of people who went through what at first appeared to be a successful life while underneath their internal software "virus" led them to do self-destructive things—people like singer Kurt Cobain of the band Nirvana, actress Marilyn Monroe, boxer Mike Tyson, Iraq's former dictator Sadam Hussein, and Germany's Adolf Hitler. And in case you're wondering, not only famous people have these problems.

In this chapter you'll learn how to recognize some of the viruses your mind may have accidentally picked up over the years. I'll also share with you some ways to overcome those negative bugs. By installing this debugging software now, you won't let those invisible viruses eat away at your good programming during the years to come. That way you can ensure you reach the levels of accomplishment you want by not sabotaging your own efforts.

Take a Test Drive

You may ask, "Is it really possible to program myself for success?" The answer is yes. However, if you think this can't be done, let's start out with a little experiment. Here's what I want you to do.

For the rest of today and tomorrow I want you to imagine you have an upset stomach and a terrible headache. Say to your self, "I feel really sick," and repeat it over and over. Say it like you mean it. Convince yourself that you are not feeling well.

Say to yourself, "My stomach feels queasy and my head is pounding." Continue doing this until, as I suspect, you will make yourself feel sick. It will happen if you follow these instructions, so go ahead and try it and see how you feel tomorrow. Stop reading right here and program yourself to feel sick.

What? You don't want to make yourself feel sick? Okay, then don't do anything I just suggested. I don't want you to follow those instructions anyway, because I know exactly what would happen. Given time, you would eventually start to experience, or imagine experiencing, some of those sickly symptoms.

Here's the point. If you believed, even slightly, that what I asked you to do would make you feel sick or even mildly uncomfortable, then you already understand the potential power of your thoughts. If you hesitated for even a single moment and said to yourself, "This guy is crazy" or "There's no way I'd do that," then at some level you realize what the power of your thoughts can be.

Likewise you would certainly understand why and how it is equally possible to use your brainpower to help program your success. Think about it. If you can make yourself feel sick, you can also make yourself feel successful. One is no different from the other except for the thoughts you think to get you there.

Realize now, if you haven't already, that you have the power to determine what you think. Your inner world, or "programming," will determine what happens in your outer world. I'm not saying you have complete control of your outer world. You can't stop a speeding car that is coming at you, but your inner world will determine how you react to that speeding car.

Your inner programming would determine whether you would run to get out of the car's way or freeze and possibly get hit. Likewise your inner world (thoughts) would dictate whether you would get angry with the crazy driver or if the nut would simply scare you. Those emotions, in turn, would dictate how you would act. Plain and simple, it's no more complicated than that.

It's All in Your Head

Let me demonstrate how this all works a bit more clearly.

Take the example of a word you know how to spell. Since we're talking about programming, let's use the word *bug*. Originally you received "input" on how to spell it. The input was probably verbal or in writing. I suspect that eventually when you saw the word *bug* the vision of a bug popped into your head. That's because words are simply representations of the real world.

If I say the word *green*, you will immediately visualize that color in your mind. If I say the word *sticky*, you'll think about some representation of that word. If I say *grizzly bear*, you form an impression of one in your head. If I say the word *success*, you immediately form a vision of what that might look like to you, and so on. Once your mind is programmed to understand a word, it immediately translates the word into an image that can be seen in the real world . . . the outer world, so to speak.

Okay, so let's go back to the bug. Get a visual image of the word *bug* in your head. Every time you think about spelling the word *bug* and write it down on paper (the external location), it will be spelled exactly the same way. Your inner world, or the picture of how you spell the word *bug* in your head, will determine your outer world . . . or how you spell the word on paper in your outer world . . . every time. Your inner world programming in your mind will always influence what happens in your outer world. Your inner world programming dictates how everything you do is perceived and created in your life.

Your mind works in the same way for everything. What your mind creates in your inner world will determine the result you create in your outer world. That's because the mind thinks in images, and you'll get what you see in your mind's eye in your outer world as well.

For example, if you repeat the same negative thoughts in your mind over and over, there is a high likelihood your life will reflect those negative thoughts in your actions. It can't help but do so, since your mind is creating an inner world picture that will create outer world results.

Eventually if your mind generates the same negative thoughts and the same negative pictures over and over again, you'll find it hard to escape the negative programming in the results you create. You will be infected by a "bug."

Focus Determines Where You Look

The first thing to understand about programming yourself for success is that your programming is determined by what you focus on, either consciously or subconsciously. How you look at things and what you focus your mental energy on will determine your programming input. It's just like looking through a camera lens. You notice what the lens is pointed at. Here's an example of what I mean.

Take a moment to look around the space you are in (room, yard, etc.) and notice everything you see that is yellow. Go ahead. Look for everything that is yellow. Now carry this book with you and leave the space you're in for just a minute. Go ahead, leave. No cheating allowed. This won't work unless you are away from the space.

Now, without looking, see if you can mentally recall everything in the space you were just in that is colored purple. Can you remember any of the purple items? At this point, feel free to go back into the space you were just in and look for the purple items.

Here's the point. Unless you know the space you were in extremely well, chances are you could remember many yellow items but few that were purple. That's because you were initially focused on looking for yellow things, not purple ones. Life works the same way.

Your mind will remember and act on whatever you tell it to focus on. For instance if you tell your mind to focus on the thought, "Why can't I meet anybody special?" your mind will answer the question you asked and find reasons in your "data bank" that would explain why you can't seem to meet anyone special. If, on the other hand, you ask your mind for solutions like, "What can I do to meet that special someone?" your mind will come up with answers to that question. Maybe not right away, but your mind will begin to process and work on finding answers for you. This all sounds very simple, and it is.

Your mind's output will always reflect the input you provide it. Your mind will focus on whatever you direct it to and just like the computer, it will retrieve information to support your request.

Please go to page 202 in your *Making Connections: Plug-It-In and Work-It-Out Tool Kit,* or log onto www.EveryAdvantage.net, and find the exercise called "Programming My Mind." With this tool you'll have an opportunity to list some of the negative questions you might be asking your mind to answer. You'll also be given an opportunity to rephrase your negative requests and input positive ones that will get your mind working in the right way to get the results you want.

Turn on the Light

Think about your conscious mind as a spotlight and your subconscious mind as a floodlight.

Like a spotlight, the conscious mind can highlight, or focus on, only one thing at a time. Your conscious mind can be aware of only a limited amount of information at one time.

A floodlight, on the other hand, can cover a wide range of things simultaneously, so your subconscious mind has continuous access to all the information that's in your head. It can locate that information to help you find answers to the questions you put into the spotlight.

If there is so much as one piece of information, one memory, that your mind can find to support a negative question, it will find it. Likewise if there is information stored that can support a positively framed question, your mind can find that as well. So it's up to you to determine where you direct the spotlight in order to get the most productive answers.

The first thing you need to master in programming your mind for success is to take control of what you focus your mind on. Simply take control of what you ask your mind to do. This isn't easy, especially if you've already developed the habits of self-doubt or self-criticism, but you can overcome it. Let's look at how.

Tuning Your Piano

Getting your new programming to "stick" in your head can be compared to tuning a new piano.

When a new piano is first tuned, it will more than likely go out of tune in a couple of days. That's because the new piano strings have a natural tendency to return to their original level of tension. To put it another way, the piano strings are "used to" being the size and shape they were prior to being stretched to tune the piano. Meanwhile the person tuning the piano is, in a sense, "asking" the strings to stretch to a certain level of tension needed to create the right musical notes. But new piano strings are pretty darn stubborn. They don't like to change.

So once the piano is first tuned, the piano strings will loosen up rather quickly. They naturally want to return to their original state of tension, and after a few days the piano will need to be tuned again.

When the piano is tuned the second time, the strings will stay in tune for perhaps a week or so. Tune it a third time and the string tension might stick for a couple of weeks, then a month, and then several months between tunings. Eventually the strings become accustomed to their new tension and don't "fight" to get back to their original state as quickly.

In the same way, as you program yourself for success, at first you will find yourself returning back to the same negative thoughts and habits you've always had. Like the piano, you'll go out of tune quickly at first and go back to your old ways of thinking. That doesn't mean your effort to change your way of thinking isn't working. You just need to tune it again and again until the new way of thinking sticks (remember perseverance!).

But instead of following through, most people simply give up. They say after the first try or two, "This just isn't working." So rather than trying again, they just quit trying, period.

Successful people learn that eventually your negative thoughts can be replaced by more productive ones, so they keep reprogramming their mind until their desired way of thinking sticks.

By the way, as you program your mind, you don't have to wait a few days or weeks between each "tuning." Instead it is a process you can and should do every day. The more you feed your mind the right programming . . . the right thoughts . . . the quicker you'll get the results you want. So make it a habit to "tune" your thoughts every day.

It's All Questions

If you understand how your mind works, you will be better prepared to program it the way you want.

The human mind is very predictable in the way it thinks. Quite simply, it thinks in questions. Yep, that's all there is to it.

From the moment you are born, your mind is curious. It's like a sponge looking to absorb as much information as it can. And in order to absorb information, your mind uses questions.

As a child everything you see, hear, feel, taste, or smell is learned by asking a question about it. You ask questions like, "What is that thing?" "What is that smell?" "What is this I'm touching?" "Why does it feel cool?" "What is this food my mom is feeding me?" "How can I get her to stop?"

Literally every time you think, your mind asks nonstop questions. "What is that?" "Do I look okay?" "What's it like outside?" "Which way do I need to turn the shower faucet to make it warmer?" "What should I do next?" "How can I do better?" "Where is that noise coming from?"

Now realize that many of these questions are asked in a split second. You don't even realize you're asking them because the brain's processing speed is so fast you often realize the answer almost immediately.

For instance, let's go back to the "colors" example we looked at earlier. If I ask you look for something in the room that is yellow, your mind will, at light speed, evaluate everything in the room until it comes upon something that is yellow. But in order to do that, your mind has to ask the question, "Is that yellow?" for each and every thing you look at until it comes up with the answer, "Yes."

This in an extremely important point to remember. Your mind will always give you answers to the questions you ask it. In other words it will look for the specific answers you ask it to find. Now it may not always immediately find the right answer, but it will always be the questions you ask your mind to answer that will determine the answers you get. Always.

So, if your mind will always look for answers to the questions you ask of it, and we can agree that you will certainly need to ask your mind questions to figure out how to be successful, then it becomes clear that **the level of success you will achieve comes down to asking the right questions.**

As we discussed earlier, if you say to yourself, "Why can't I do that?" you'll get a different answer than if you ask, "How can I get that done?"

Instead of asking, "What's wrong with me?" ask, "What's good about me?" Instead of asking, "How come I can't decide on what I want to do with my life?" ask, "What can I do to help me decide on what I want to do with my life?"

Ask the right questions and your mind will help you find the answers you are looking for. Ask the wrong questions and your mind will be happy to give you answers to those questions as well. So get your mind focused on productive thoughts and ask it to answer productive questions.

You Get What You Expect

Let's switch gears and discuss another concept that will impact the results you get.

It's been said, "You don't get what you want in life. You get what you expect." As a general rule that is true. Over time you'll get exactly what you expect of your personal actions, abilities, and situations, because you will create the environment to get the results you expect. From time to time you may get a few surprises that conflict with this truth, but over time you will get the results you expect to get.

During the daytime it's light outside and during the night it's dark, right? Well, sort of. That statement is almost always true, but if you're in the North Pole during the winter, it is dark all day during part of the year. Likewise in the South Pole it's light all day during that same time.

My point is that there are always exceptions, but given the option of operating under the rule of expectations or not, you're going to be right 99% of the time if you go with the rule that you'll get what you expect. So focus on this rule, and not on the possible exceptions, and the numbers will be in your favor.

There was famous classroom study done in 1964 and 1965 by Dr. Robert Rosenthal, a Harvard University psychologist, and Lenore Jacobsen, a San Francisco elementary school principal. They asked the question, "Do some children perform poorly in school because their teachers expect them to?"

If that is true, they predicted that raising the teachers' expectations of how well the children could do should raise the children's performance as well. So they gave a group of kindergarten through fifth-grade students a learning ability test and tabulated the results.

The next fall the new teachers were given the names of 5 or 6 children in their classroom who, because of their results on this test, were identified as supposedly having exceptional learning ability. However, the teachers didn't know that the test results were actually rigged and that these so-called "exceptional students" were chosen randomly.

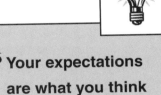

At the end of the school year all the children were retested, and some astonishing results were realized. The students whom the teachers thought had the most potential actually scored far ahead of the other kids and gained as many as 15 to 27 I.Q. (intelligence quotient) points on the test. In addition the teachers described these children as happier, more affectionate than average, more curious, and having a better chance of success in later life.

> **❝ Your expectations are what you think will happen, and your actions will always support your thinking so that you get the outcome you expect. ❞**

Why did that happen? It happened because the teachers expected these "smarter" students to do better, and so their actions in teaching these supposed smarter kids supported their expectation.

Think about that true story and you'll begin to understand why you get what you expect in life. The mind doesn't like to be wrong, so it works at not being wrong.

If you focus a camera on a certain scene, the scene is what you will get when the picture develops. Likewise when your expectations are what you focus on, the result your mind "sees" happening is what you'll get when the situation "develops." Let's look at an example.

Say there's someone you really want to hang out with, and you're considering asking him or her to do that. What eventually will happen depends to a great degree on what your mind expects to happen. That's because you'll take actions that are consistent with the picture of the expectation your mind generates.

If you expect that person to say "no" to your invitation to hang out, there's a good chance that you may not even ask him or her in the first place, right? So in this case your expectation will be exactly what you get. You anticipated a "no" answer, so you didn't extend an invitation to hang out and, therefore by default, got a "no" answer.

Now suppose you think that same person *might* want to hang out with you, so you get up the nerve to ask her or him. You'd probably handle your proposal in one of two ways. First you might approach the individual with some level of doubt, as if you expect to be turned down. What do you think would happen if you came off that way? Yep, there's a good chance you'd get the cold shoulder. Your expectation of rejection could be the deciding factor as to whether he or she would agree to spend some time with you.

But suppose the tone in your voice and your approach to asking him or her were confident. You'd stand a much better chance of getting a "yes," because the only way to truly seem confident is if you are, in fact, confident. And you'd act that way, because you'd expect that there is a chance he or she would agree to hang with you. It's sort of a self-fulfilling prophecy.

So your expectations impact your confidence in something happening, and your confidence in something happening will support your expectations. They go together.

Sometimes it's hard to see or understand that your expectation of something happening will directly influence the outcome, but in life it's all how you look at things. Your point of view, how you see and interpret things, is your truth. So to change your truth, you must change your point of view. You must change what you expect.

What "Shoe" Thinking?

There's a story about two salespeople who went to a remote area of Africa to evaluate the sales potential of the marketplace. Their company was in the business of making and selling shoes. One of the two salespeople really didn't want to make the trip. He was convinced there was no opportunity to sell shoes in that part of Africa. Guess what happened?

After visiting and examining the situation, this doubtful salesperson wrote back about his conclusion to his company, "I've evaluated the market potential and, as I suspected, see no opportunity to sell any shoes here. In fact nobody even wears shoes."

The second salesperson did want to make the trip to explore the potential, since she expected that there might be a good opportunity to sell shoes in this area of the continent. After arriving at the destination and making a short observation, she e-mailed back her message, which was vastly different from the other salesperson's. The second salesperson wrote, "As I thought, there is a huge opportunity here. You won't believe this, but nobody currently even has shoes." Of course she went on to sell a record number of shoes to this new market.

The bottom line is that you are more likely to get what you expect, because your expectations influence how you approach a situation which, in turn, influences your actions. When your mind is focused on a mental image of what you expect to happen, your dominant thoughts will taint your opinion and view of the situation, which will direct the actions you take. It's that simple.

Some people thought the truth was that the Internet would never take off, but it was the people who did have the expectation of what the Internet would become who have brought it to where it is today. Their expectations impacted their actions, like the creation of Google, AOL, E-Bay, and Yahoo! among others.

If what you expect to happen influences what you will do, you can understand why people who didn't expect the Internet ever to become much of anything probably didn't benefit much from its development. Those people didn't see any practical reason to do anything to take advantage of the Internet, because they didn't expect anything to come of it.

So your expectations about your life will influence the actions you take and will therefore move you toward creating the life you expect.

What are some of the expectations you have that support your success? What are some that don't support your success? List 5 of each on the next page. (Hint: Examples might include, "I expect to get good grades" or "I expect to get poor grades;" "I expect to make the team" or "I expect not to make the team.")

(**Note:** If this book belongs to someone else or to a library, please do this exercise on a *separate* sheet of paper.)

Supporting Expectations

1) _____

2) _____

3) _____

4) _____

5) _____

Self-Limiting Expectations

1) _____

2) _____

3) _____

4) _____

5) _____

How might you do things differently if your expectation about these issues changes? What actions would you be likely to take? How would you change your outlook if you expected a different outcome? How might people treat you differently if your expectations were different?

According to futurist Daniel Burrus, "How you view the future shapes your actions today, and your actions today will literally shape your future. Your future view will determine the future you." So how do you create a productive future view that you can expect to happen . . . a view that creates the future you want?

Move Toward Your Desired Outcome

One key is not to focus on the ultimate outcome, but rather focus on moving *toward* the desired outcome (remember, success is a process). You need to program your thinking so that you clearly understand that you simply need to make some form of progress.

If you say, "I want to get straight A's this next semester" and you currently get mostly B's and C's, perhaps you should focus on an outcome that you are more likely to be successful at . . . an outcome you have a reasonable expectation of achieving. That might be as simple as shooting for straight B's, or A's and B's, or A's in certain classes.

The important thing is to make sure you don't overwhelm yourself and set yourself up for failure. If you pick one class to get an A, you'll probably be able to focus enough time and energy on that class so you can expect to get an A. If you can focus enough to reasonably expect an A, chances are very good you will achieve it.

Momentum Will Get You Going

In order to get any ball rolling, you must give it an initial push. Once you get a ball rolling, it's much easier to keep it rolling.

If you want to lose 10 pounds, you must first put together a plan to achieve the objective. In fact your plan should start with losing just one pound. Once you have a plan, your expectations for achieving the objective will get much stronger. Your programming is more likely to stick since your plan supports your programming.

The first thing you must decide to do when programming yourself for success is exactly what you want to see happen. What are the ideal outcomes you want? Once you identify those outcomes, you'll be able to effectively use the concepts we've discussed here to program your thinking.

Review

1. Your input "programming" comes from a wide range of sources, and as a young child you have little control over what is programmed.
2. It is possible to use your brainpower to help program your success.
3. What your mind creates in your inner world will determine the result you get in your outer world.
4. Your programming is determined by what you focus on, either consciously or subconsciously.
5. Your mind will focus on whatever you direct it to and, like a computer, it will retrieve information to support your request. When you ask your mind productive questions, it will try to give you productive answers.
6. You can program your mind like tuning a piano.
7. Successful people learn that their negative thoughts eventually will be displaced by more productive ones, so they keep reprogramming their minds until their desired way of thinking sticks.
8. We think in questions, and success comes down to asking the right questions so that your mind will look for the right answers.
9. Your expectations are what you think will happen, and your actions will always support your thinking and increase the likelihood that you get the outcome you expect.
10. Expectations create a self-fulfilling prophecy, and your expectations about your life will do the same.

"Program" Yourself for Success
Computer Viruses of the Mind

> When you finish this chapter, you'll:
>
> ◆ Have learned more ways to make your mind work for you.
> ◆ Take away some ideas on how you can better manage things like worries, anger, and procrastination.

Now that we've explored how the mind is programmed and how it really works, we'll cover some of the most common negative programs. I call them viruses of the mind. These little "bugs" can sit in the core of your thinking and impact how you look at and process information.

In this chapter you'll learn how to detect each virus, and we'll explore some of the most powerful positive programs you can "install" to help you debug your system and reach unlimited success.

The Worry Bug

The first virus is what I call "The Worry Bug." I'll refer to him as "WB" for short.

WB is an interesting little critter. His primary objective is to keep you focused on one word . . . *could*. In other words WB's big question is, "What could go wrong with a situation?" As we just discussed, once WB asks that question, your mind tries to answer it, of course.

WB feeds on your fear, and much of your fear is based on a sense that you don't have sufficient control over a situation. Worry is always based on the possibility of something happening in the future. That creates a little something called anxiety.

WB knows the more you worry . . . the more you'll worry. The Worry Bug wants you to get on this endless merry-go-round so that you can't get off. WB doesn't want you to focus on solutions, just on potential problems. It's a vicious cycle. Worry breeds more worry, and that's what WB likes.

WB knows that there are solutions out there, but that if you find them, you will eliminate him. So to survive WB has to keep you occupied with unproductive worries that keep you away from focusing on solutions. That's the way he survives. Your worries are his food.

So again, the basis of all worry is the word *could*. It's all about what "could" happen.

Worry is a form of fear, and fear is driven by the possibility of loss—loss of pride, loss of power or loss of control, according to Dr. David Viscott, author of *Taking Risks—How to Conquer the Fears that Hold You Back*. You may be interested to know that the verb *worry* actually meant "to strangle" or "to choke" in its earliest usage. The original word was "wyrgeth" in Old English. And just like the word's origin, the Worry Bug can "choke" off your logical mind causing you to see things differently than they really are. The expression "he choked" is often associated with someone who had been worrying.

When we think about what "could" happen, we're turning our attention to the unknown and focusing on the most negative outcome (or expectation) possible. Variations of the word *could* include "might," "may," and "what if," to name a few. These are the words that can keep you focused on worries, because they leave open the possibility of something bad happening. They leave open a reason to have fear.

Some negative worry programming may have been downloaded when you were a little kid. You may have heard adults say things like, "Don't do that. You could get hurt." Or a friend may have said, "We could get in trouble for doing that" or "Think about what might have happened if I didn't stop you." You've probably heard far fewer phrases like, "Keep doing that. You could be successful at it" or "You may just be right."

Oddly enough, most worries are completely unfounded and unnecessary. According to Earl Nightingale, author of *Lead the Field,* the following are estimates of what people actually worry about. I think you'll find these statistics interesting.

Things People Worry About	Percent of Total Worries
—Things that never actually happen	40%
—Things over and gone that can never be changed	30%
—Needless worries about your health	12%
—Petty miscellaneous worries	10%
—Real legitimate worries	8%

As you can see, 92% of the average person's worries are completely unproductive, take up a lot of important time, and cause stress, so these false worries are totally unnecessary.

The conscious mind is like the shelves at a grocery store. There is only so much space available at any one time. Like the grocery shelf, if you want to give more space to cornflakes, you have to take some space away from raisin bran or oatmeal.

Unlike your subconscious mind, which has unlimited space, your conscious mind has only so much shelf space. In other words you can only consciously think of a limited number of things at any one time. So if you use up your conscious "shelf space" stocking worries, you'll have less room to stock solutions or productive thoughts.

So what worries are worth worrying about? Of real legitimate worries there are only two types:

1. The kinds of problems we can solve.
2. The kinds of problems that are beyond our ability to solve personally.

Most real worries fall into the first group. We can solve them, but because we often spend our time worrying rather than on problem solving, WB is going to get exactly what he wants. Namely, we end up focusing (asking our questions) on the worry and never come to a solution. And if we don't find a solution, we continue to worry. Smart guy, that WB. But you can beat him at his own game.

Beating the Worry Bug

If you are infected with the WB, the first thing you need to know to beat the little critter is how to recognize a worry when one pops in your head. You may think this is obvious, but the fact is that the WB can get you so wrapped up in your worry that you don't even stop to think, "Hey, this is a worry I'm experiencing here."

 Worries are pretty easy to spot, and here's how to recognize one. **Whenever you feel uneasy about anything, you are enjoying a little visit from the WB.**

As mentioned earlier, worry involves essentially one thing: the possibility of a loss of some sort. It can be the loss of power or control including the control of material items, the loss of love or affection, or the loss of who you are as a person, your self-esteem.

When you are uneasy or worried about something, it's important to pause and understand exactly what is worrying you. Until you realize what it is that you're worried about, you really can't do anything about the worry.

When you feel uneasy and realize that WB has shown its ugly head, consider the following:

1. First, ask yourself if there is anything going on in your life

that could involve the potential loss of power, control, love, or your self-image? Once you recognize what you might be worried about . . .

2. Ask yourself if it is a real, legitimate worry or are you just worrying because it makes you feel like you're at least doing something about whatever the situation is? Sometimes people worry because it makes them feel like they're taking some sort of action regarding their worry. But worrying itself doesn't change anything.

3. Is it a worry or just a simple concern? There is a distinct difference between "worry" and "concern." Concern is something you are interested in, something that has drawn your attention and is worth thinking about. Concern involves a more level-headed interest in a situation, and it is characterized less by potential feelings of loss than is worry. Concern is not as intense as worry, because concern gives you a little more confidence that you can actually do something about the situation. But because worry puts the focus on potential loss, it can cause anxiety and stress and so foster the feeling that you cannot do anything to change what's going on.

4. Are you worrying about something you have no control over? One example may be that you are worried that that special person may not call you tonight.

Here's the reality. That person either is going to call or he or she isn't. All the worrying in the world won't change that, because you have no control over whether the person calls or not. And if you have no control to begin with, you haven't lost any control.

If your worry is about something you have no control over, change your worry to an expectation and you won't feel so let down. In this situation, for instance, you would change the thought of worry to, "I know there's a chance that special person may not call tonight." Then, if he or she does, you'll be pleasantly surprised, and if you don't get the call, well, you knew they might not call anyway.

If you change your worry into an expectation, you move on and are able to do something about it. For example, let's say I'm having a party in my backyard tonight and am worried it is going to rain. All the possible worrying I can muster up will not change the weather. But if I simply expect it to rain, my expectation creates a concern that I can act on. I will probably do something about the party like moving it inside the house or rescheduling it altogether. Now I am in control.

Realize that the thing you are worrying about will either happen or it won't, and all the worrying in the world won't change the eventual outcome. Only action can change an outcome.

Be sure to remember that 92% of all worries won't happen or are based on events in the past that cannot be changed or are needless worries about health or are petty and not worth your time.

Since most worries will never amount to anything, you need to stay focused on what you can do to reduce the possibility of your legitimate worries from occurring.

All You Can Do Is All You Can Do—So Do it!

When I give speeches or seminars, I often ask the group this question: "If the speed of light is 286,000 miles per second, then what is the fastest speed that light can travel?"

The answer, of course, is 286,000 miles per second. The light goes as fast as it can. It can't physically go any faster. There is a natural limit to its speed.

The next question I ask is, "What is the most you can do about anything?" The answer is, of course, "The most you can do is the most you can do."

After you do all you can do, you've done what you can to affect the outcome of an event. So if you choose to worry about something, you must take your best shot at fixing the problem. If you can fix it, you will fix it. If you can't, you won't, so stop worrying and move on. It's not worth your time. Don't let the Worry Bug take control of your mind. You need to take control.

The next thing you can do to deprogram the WB virus is to fool him into giving you answers he doesn't want to hear. So instead of focusing on what "could" happen that is bad, ask yourself and focus on what positive result could happen. That'll really throw WB for a loop!

You Never Know

There is a story of an older man who lived in Europe several hundred years ago. He lived on a farm with his wife and adult son. One day his son was doing some farm work during a critical part of the growing season, and he fell and broke his leg. A neighbor who saw what happened approached the older man and said, "It is unfortunate what happened to your son." The older man replied, "It is neither fortunate nor unfortunate. It just is."

The very next day some soldiers came by the house to take the young man to war. Seeing he had a broken leg, they moved on and let him be.

Having seen these events too, the neighbor came to the house again and said, "You are fortunate that your son did not have to go to war." The older man replied, "It is neither fortunate nor unfortunate. It just is."

A few days later the soldiers came marching by, each survivor carrying large sums of gold and jewels confiscated from the enemy they'd just defeated.

Several days later the older man was plowing the corn fields himself when the plow horse snapped loose from the harness and ran away. The neighbor once again came over and said, "It is unfortunate that your one and only plow horse has run away." Again the older man replied, "It is neither fortunate nor unfortunate. It just is." A week later the horse came running back to the farm leading a half dozen wild horses with him.

The neighbor came by again and said, "You are very fortunate to have so many strong horses." The older man responded, "It is neither fortunate nor unfortunate. It just is." After several days the older man discovered that the horses had trampled the very cornfield he had just planted, ruining the potential harvest.

The message here is that rarely is anything in life what it seems to be. When you think there is a problem, it often turns out that there isn't one. And when you believe all is going well, something can happen to ruin it. So don't waste your time worrying about uncontrollable or trite events. Remember that 92% of worries are over things that never happen, things you can't change anyway, or other petty things not worth worrying about.

Things will be as things will be. Just do what you can do about them, and that is all you can do.

Please go to page 204 in your *Making Connections: Plug-It-In and Work-*

It-Out Tool Kit, or log onto www.EveryAdvantage.net, and find the "My Worry Profile." It's a short exercise that will help you determine how much of a worrier you are or aren't. You can think of it as your Worry Bug virus scan.

Beating the Bug

When you catch yourself worrying, try the following exercise. This is an exercise you should do with your eyes closed. It may help to ask someone to read this to you while your eyes are closed or you can read the exercise first and then do it. If you have speakers on your PC, you may find it more effective to use the audio version on www.EveryAdvantage.net. Just click on "Beat the Bug," and I'll guide you through it.

With your eyes closed, create an image in your mind of the outcome you are worried about. Let's say you're worried about failing an upcoming test, so you'd start by picturing yourself taking the test.

Next think about the specific worry you are having. In this example you might create a mental picture of your teacher handing you a poor test score.

Okay, now let's take some power away from the WB! In your mind make the image of your teacher handing you the poor score a black and white "picture" instead of in color. Now very slowly shrink the black and white image down very small. Smaller. Smaller. Got it? Good. Now from behind your back, grab an imaginary sledgehammer. Pull the hammer back and slam it down on the image that worries you. Slam it a few times if you want. You should feel the worry decrease, since you have taken control of the worry and smashed it. You have diminished the WB's power, because you have given yourself the power to destroy the defeating thought.

If the same worry crops up again, and it's very possible that it will, do the same exercise and imagine that you're driving a steamroller over the problem.

Here's why this will work. When you shrink the image of the worry in your mind, take away the color of reality, and destroy the image in some way, your subconscious programming will begin to see you defeating the worry. Like the piano strings being tuned, if you visualize this enough, ultimately the worry will be reduced or eliminated. It really works. Try it a few times and you'll see what I mean.

Other ways to trash a worry include:

◆ See the worry on a mirror or piece of glass and shatter it.
◆ Imagine the worry is a balloon and pop it.
◆ Pretend the worry is on a punching bag and beat the #@*! out of it.
◆ Visualize the worry as a piece of paper and burn it.
◆ See the worry on a feather, and let the wind blow it away.

You get the idea. Just think of a way to dull, shrink, and obliterate the image and you'll find this a great tool to help you reduce a worry.

Plant Your Feet

Here's another way to help you minimize worries. Since worry is all about what might happen in the future, it will help you if you can keep your focus on the present. A great way to do that is simply to feel your feet planted firmly on the floor or your hands firmly on a table (remember the awareness exercise in an earlier chapter?). By feeling where you are right now, it will help reinforce the feeling that you are here in the present. And if you feel like you're in the present, you will be less concerned about the future.

This stuff may seem unusual, but it works because you are sending a message to your subconscious mind that you are here in the present and are in control.

But If You Must Worry . . .

There will be times when you say, "Hey, this is one I really do need to, or want to, worry about." When that happens, and it will, try the following:

1) Decide how much time you will give yourself to find a solution to the worry. Don't make your deadline too short. Just define a specific amount of time you'll commit to the worry.

Worries frequently turn out to be unimportant, while they seem urgent. Remember, important things aren't necessarily urgent, and urgent things aren't always important.

You'll discover that putting a limit on how much you worry about something doesn't change the outcome. **Nothing in your life will change purely because you worry about it. You can only change something by *acting* on it.**

2) Ask yourself, "What is one possible good outcome that can come from this thing I'm worrying about?" For example, if you are worried about passing a certain test, ask yourself how you would feel if you actually aced it. This will tell your subconscious that all is not lost and will help tone down the worry. You may have to dig down to think of a possible positive outcome, but there is always one there.

3) Ask yourself, "What is the worst possible outcome of this thing I'm worrying about?" For instance, you may realize that the worst possible outcome of failing a test is that you will get only a C in the class. Put that into perspective since getting a C is certainly better than flunking the class. Often the worst thing is only a temporary inconvenience or is minor compared to other things. So it helps to keep things in perspective.

4) Another unusual thing you can do is put a loose rubber band around your wrist. Whenever you find yourself worrying, snap the rubber band. This little sting will start to train your mind that in order to avoid the sting it needs to avoid worrying. This can work for you only if you are willing to snap the rubber band, because your mind will train itself to do whatever it takes to avoid the pain.

Okay, enough talk about WB. You've learned some practical tools to help you keep that annoying little bugger under control. Now it's time to learn about WB's equally destructive cousin, H2.

The Hot Head Virus

The second common destructive virus is the Hot Head virus. I call him "H2." This nasty guy's purpose is similar to its cousin's, the Worry Bug, except while WB wants to keep you feeling scared, H2 wants to keep you feeling angry.

Anger and resentment can create their own set of problems if you let them flourish in your personal programming. When you get angry, you tend to focus on the anger, and anger, like worry, feeds itself. It fuels its own fire.

It's normal to get angry about some things, but a strong H2 virus causes you to react with anger to almost anything you think isn't exactly the way it should be. H2 simply puts you closer to the edge.

Just as the root word of worry is *could*, according to Dr. Denis Waitley, noted psychologist and author of *How to Handle Conflict and Manage Anger*, the root word of all anger, without exception, is the word *should*. An example might be when you get angry with someone who cuts in front of you while you are waiting in line for a movie or at the grocery checkout. Believe it or not, it isn't the fact that they cut in line that makes you angry. Instead you're angry because they shouldn't have done it.

Think about it. If that same person was blind and didn't see you, or if it were a little three-year-old child, you'd probably not think much of his cutting in line. You'd figure that he just didn't know any better. But the fact is he still committed the act of cutting in line, right? So it's not really what someone does that makes us angry. Instead we get angry when we think an act should or should not have occurred.

When you get mad at a friend who didn't call you back as promised, it isn't the fact that she didn't call that is the issue. Instead you are angry because you think she "should" have kept her promise. If you later learn that your friend didn't call because she was in a bad car accident or had a death in the family, the fact that she didn't call you still exists, but your anger would go away because you now understand that there was no "should."

When you get angry with yourself for doing something stupid, it isn't what you do that makes you angry. Rather you are angry with yourself because you know you shouldn't have done it. If you later find out that what you did wasn't so stupid after all, the "shouldn't" part of the equation goes away. And so does the anger. Interesting, huh?

Simply stated, anger is based on a point of view that something should or should not occur.

Your point of view represents your opinion of whether something should or shouldn't be. People seriously affected by the H2 virus tend to see the world as working against them. More things trigger their anger because they look at more things from the standpoint of how they believe they should be—the way they ought to be in their opinion.

As with the Worry Bug's "could," the H2's "should" takes your thinking out of the present. In the present things are just the way they are. So "should" is not an issue because what is just is. But when "should" enters the scene, it takes you off center in that you believe the situation should be different, so you feel justified in being angry. In other words, like the Worry Bug, the Hot Head virus takes you off balance. He causes you to use your energy to think about how something "should" be rather than staying balanced and realizing that things are just the way they are. If you go through life letting H2 get the best of you, you will not be in control of your life. The Hot Head will.

Since the word *should* is really a matter of opinion, if you can simply change your way of thinking about situations, you may be able to limit your anger. And as we reviewed earlier, asking yourself constructive questions can help. Here are examples of what I mean.

1. People affected by the H2 virus think like this:
   She should not have cut in front of me. That pisses me off.

   While people who can overcome the H2 virus think this way:
   I wonder what kind of hurry she's in that caused her to cut in front of me.

2. People contaminated by the H2 virus think like this:
   I can't believe it. He told me he'd call me back. He should have kept his word.

   While people who can overcome the H2 virus think this way:
   I wonder what happened that caused my friend to break his promise and not call me back. I hope he's okay.

3. People contaminated by the H2 virus think like this:
   I shouldn't have done something so stupid.

   While people who can overcome the H2 virus think this way:
   That's not like me. I wonder what made me do that.

When you begin to realize that many of the "shoulds" in life are out of your control and that the world is not just out to annoy or persecute you, you begin to think of these sorts of incidents as being just the way things happen sometimes rather than as a personal attack on your principles.

Please go to page 209 in your *Making Connections: Plug-It-In and Work-It-Out Tool Kit,* or log onto www.EveryAdvantage.net to find a short personal virus scan called "The Hot Head Virus Scan." You'll find it a useful tool that can help you determine if you are infected by H2.

The Putitoff Bug

Welcome back. Let's move on to the next "virus" of the mind. I call this guy "Comrade Putitoff."

It sounds like a Russian name, but the Putitoff Bug has nothing to do with "rushin'." In fact this bug gets exactly the opposite result. Putitoff is all about procrastination and putting things off until the future. (We discussed procrastination a bit earlier.)

Putitoff's sole mission is to keep you from doing things you should be doing. This guy is related to the Worry Bug in that procrastination is a form of fear—fear of having to deal with something or the possible outcome that something can create.

You see, if you put off doing something, then you don't have to face it, and if you don't have to face it, you can't fail at it. Likewise, if you are afraid of success, procrastinating ensures you won't have to deal with being successful either.

Procrastination is not simply about delaying things or deciding to do something later. There can be logical reasons for doing those things. Instead, procrastination is the act of not taking action because you don't want to deal with that action at the present time.

So, for example, if you need to do some homework but accidentally don't bring home the right book from school, you might have to put off doing that assignment. In this case, though, you'd be delaying doing the work because you didn't have the right resource available. That's a logical reason and is not driven by your not wanting to do it.

On the other hand if you have an assignment to do but decide you really don't feel like doing it and would rather watch your favorite TV show, you would be procrastinating. That's because you would be delaying doing something you should do in favor of something else. Putitoff makes you pick the distraction rather than take the action needed to accomplish something.

The Putitoff Bug is an expert at helping you come up with excuses for not doing the things you need to do. He can keep you from starting or from finishing something, because he creates the illusion that the thing you need to do is either of little interest to you, beyond your ability to do, or will in some way cause you discomfort or pain.

If you find yourself putting off what you know you should be doing, think about these questions:

- Why am I procrastinating? What am I afraid will happen if I follow through and actually do this thing?
- What will I gain from procrastinating? Is it enough to motivate me to do so?
- What will I lose by procrastinating? Is it enough to move me to take action?
- What will I gain by getting it over and done with?
- Can I begin by taking just one step toward doing this rather than feeling like I need to complete it fully?

This last bullet is a great tool to help you stop procrastinating about something. Taking some form of action will help create the momentum needed to follow through and do it. It often takes the most energy just to get the ball rolling, but once you do, things start to flow for you.

One example I can give you from my personal experience is when I know I need to work out but am soooooo comfortable just lying on the couch and watching TV. I simply don't want to get up, so I channel surf trying to put off the inevitable. When that happens, sometimes I just force myself to do nothing more than stand up (you know the feeling). Just the act of standing up gets me into the mode of taking action. Once I get up, I've begun the momentum needed to put on my workout clothes and get going with my exercise.

So, to end this chapter, I recommend that you pick one thing you've been procrastinating about and just do it. You'll be amazed at how much better you'll feel by simply getting on with it.

Review

1. The Worry Bug (WB) focuses your mind on what "could" go wrong with a situation.
2. Only 8% of our worries are real and legitimate. They are:
   a. The kinds of problems you can solve.
   b. The kinds of problems that are beyond your ability to solve personally.
3. Remember to use visual imagery to obliterate whatever is worrying you.
4. The Hot Head virus (H2) focuses your mind on the word *should*. Remember that whether something should or shouldn't be is just a point of view.
5. Try reframing a "should" into a positive question for your mind to answer.
6. The Putitoff Bug's sole mission is to keep you from doing things you really ought to be doing, so remember to take at least the first step and just get your momentum going.
7. Procrastination is the act of not taking action, because you do not want to deal with that action at the present time.

FlashPoint

Setting and Achieving
Your Personal Goals

When you finish this chapter, you'll:

◆ Understand what a personal goal is and what it isn't.
◆ Know about the different areas of life for which you'll consider setting goals.
◆ Know how to create personal goals that will work for you.
◆ See why having personal goals is critical to achieving the success you want.
◆ Know why *why* is such an important word.
◆ Understand why you'll want to have balance in your life.

Scoring with Goals

Personal goal setting may be the most often covered subject in the area of personal development. There's a reason for that: the ability to set meaningful personal goals is critical to attaining the highest levels of success in life. Oddly enough, however, only a small fraction of people ever learn how to set and achieve their personal goals, and an even smaller fraction actually follow up and take action on their goal setting plan. This explains why a very small percentage of people are considered highly successful in any particular area of life.

The reason that so few people set and pursue well-thought-out personal goals isn't because they don't want to. Rather it's because most people don't understand the importance of this practice. In addition few people have formally learned how to set goals. The public education system simply doesn't provide much, if any, formal curriculum in the areas of personal development. It isn't set up to do that.

Sure, we should be able to read and write and do math when we graduate high school, but typical schooling provides us very little, if any, training on how to manage our lives successfully. Good news though. You'll find that setting and pursuing personal goals will be one of the most effective things you can do to help you manage your life.

So What Exactly Is a Personal Goal?

A personal goal is not simply something you'd like to do, nor is it something you want to have. It's true that those are characteristics of a good personal goal, but just "liking" or "wanting" something does not make it a personal goal.

In the simplest terms, a true "personal goal" is a specific outcome that you are committed to achieving and are willing to support with a plan and action. A goal is a clearly defined accomplishment or milestone you can aim for and is something you can describe in vivid detail. A goal creates a target for you, just like in archery, basketball, hockey, or whatever other sport example you can think of.

The importance of a goal, whether it is in sports or in life, is that without a goal, without a target, without a defined point you want to reach, you will never know how you are doing on your success journey. You'll never know because you won't have a clear idea of what you are aiming for. And if you don't know what you're aiming for, how will you know "it" if you see it?

Without a goal it is very difficult to measure what you've achieved. Consider the game of American football. There is a clearly defined term known as a "touchdown." A touchdown occurs when the offense of a football team carries the ball across the "goal line" into what is known as the "end zone." The team then has the opportunity to score an extra point by kicking the football in between the uprights of the "goalpost." When both of these things happen, the team is said to have scored a goal and the extra point.

So the question is, when this happens, has the football team successfully achieved its goal? You won't be surprised to hear that the answer is both yes and no.

In professional football, for example, the ultimate goal for the team is to win a Super Bowl ring, but in order to do so the team must first win the Super Bowl championship game. Prior to winning the Super Bowl, the goal of the team must be to win its division championship so that it can play in the Super Bowl. In order to win the division championship, the goal prior to that must be to make the playoffs. And in order to make the playoffs, the team's goal must be to achieve a winning record that is among the best in its division.

To attain that goal of a winning record, the team members must have the goal of winning each individual game they play. In order to win every game they possibly can, they must have the goals of scoring as many points as they can in each game while holding their opponents to as few points as possible. But it doesn't stop there.

In order to achieve the goal of scoring points, the offense needs to set goals throughout its possession of the ball in order to earn first downs, or travel at least 10 yards forward on each possession. In order to travel those 10 yards, the team must establish plays to accomplish smaller goals, some of which are just to travel a few yards closer to the first down marker.

Likewise the defense must have the goal of stopping the opposing team's offense from scoring a touchdown or field goal. In order to do that, the defense must have the goal of keeping the offense from achieving first downs, and to accomplish that they must have a goal to stop the offense from gaining any ground on each and every play. You get the idea.

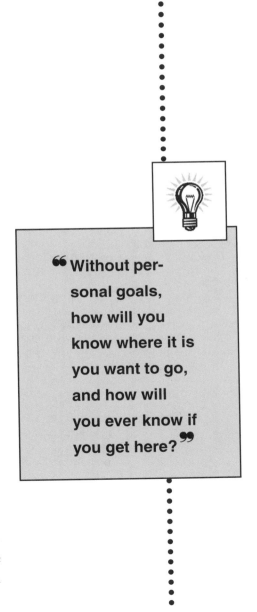

❝Without personal goals, how will you know where it is you want to go, and how will you ever know if you get here?❞

With all that said, how many potential goals could you count in the paragraphs above? A lot, I'll bet. That's because **a goal is not necessarily an ultimate destination or an end result alone. Rather a goal can consist of a series of outcomes or results you need to reach in order to progress to a defined ending outcome, or the "master" goal.** Sounds a bit like the definition of success, doesn't it?

If the football players in this example had only one goal, to win the Super Bowl, and didn't have subgoals to get them there, what is the chance that they would ever get to the big game? The answer is "diddly-squat." Without a planned sequence of progressive goals to achieve, they would never get to the top of their game. And the same applies to each of us in the game of life.

Why Is a Goal Needed?

Step back for a moment. What would happen if there were no goals in football? I mean, literally no goals, as in the football team didn't know where the goal line was or even where the first down markers were? What if there was no defined direction in which to go? In other words there was no identifiable goal or predetermined direction in which to move. How would the players know which direction to go? How would they know if they were achieving first downs? How would they know if they were playing successfully? The answer is, they wouldn't.

Without knowing what you are aiming for, and without defining the outcome you are working toward, how will you know if you ever achieve anything worthwhile? Likewise without having specific goals for your life, all you'd have left are chaos and random outcomes created through random events.

If you don't have a defined place to go, a defined outcome, how will you know when or if you get there? You won't because there is no "there" to get to.

In the example the football team technically could go on playing the game forever, but without a defined goal, they would be unable to define success. That's because they wouldn't know what success was supposed to look like. Essentially they would be lost because they wouldn't know in which direction to run. And even if they had a sense for the right direction, they would never know if they achieved anything, because there were no goals, or milestones, in place to let them know.

Suppose the football team gets near the invisible goal . . . near the "pay-off" . . . but doesn't know it. When this happens, the chances that the team would just give up increase dramatically, because they'd have no idea that they are as close to the goal as they are. They'd have no defined goal to let them know how close they are to a touchdown. Without that defined goal there is no clear indicator of success. Success stays ambiguous.

Not having clearly defined personal goals is one of the most common characteristics of those who don't achieve much in life. After all, how can they achieve anything if they have nothing clearly defined to achieve? And even if they do achieve something by accident, how will they know they've achieved anything if there is no benchmark for achievement?

If you want to achieve high levels of success in life, you must first iden-tify what success means to you. (I've already offered my definition of success in a previous chapter and you've created your own as well). Then you must define the intermediate, or subgoals, required to move you closer to your ultimate goal. Finally, you will need to take action.

It's incredible how many people wander through life without clear goals. They simply do things that "feel" right and see what the result is, hoping it is something they can live with. They don't necessarily have a defined result that they are shooting for, even something that they can picture in their heads. Rather they take actions that feel good at the time and just hope that all comes out well. Do you know anyone like that? Do you know any-body who simply goes through the motions and hopes that things turn out in his or her favor? I'll bet you do.

Here's a fact. What I just described is how most people live their lives. In fact you might even say that most people let their lives live them. They go along for the ride but don't put a plan together to get anywhere specific. Instead they go through life unhappy working for, or following, those who do have a plan.

> **❝You might say that most people let their lives live them.❞**

Your goal plan is your roadmap, your visual reminder of what you want to achieve. It will be your reference point you can go back to over and over not only to remind you of what you want, but also to help you keep a clear picture in your mind of what you are trying to accomplish. Your goals add direction to your life. They are the clearly defined targets you are aiming for.

That all said, it's important to understand that, just like when using a roadmap when you are driving, in life you can't always anticipate everything that might occur down the road. So although your goals will be a valuable roadmap for you, you should realize that you may not always want to stick so strictly to the initial map that you don't notice the changes. A map is simply a starting point that heads you in the right direction. Sometimes things will change, making sense for you to rewrite portions of your map. Goals can change.

I Need Some Directions

Have you ever had someone call you and ask for directions to your house or to your friend's party or wherever? Sure you have. What do you tell him?

I'm sure you'll agree that in order to give him or her good directions you need to know two things. First you need to know where he is. Then you need to know where he wants to end up. Only with both of those pieces of information can you get him to where he wants to go.

Goal setting does the same thing for you. It helps you understand where you are now and where you want to go regarding a specific accomplishment. And just like when you give someone directions (i.e., go two blocks and turn left on Casey Street and then go three miles and turn right on Smith, and so on), the goal setting system you'll learn here will help you figure out where you are in relationship to a goal, where you eventually want to be, and what "intersections" or subgoals you will need to accomplish to get there.

Solving Life's Puzzle

Okay. It's time to do a short exercise that will provide you with a fun and simple demonstration of the importance of having clearly defined, written goals in life. You can also find a copy of this puzzle called "Solving Life's Puzzle" on www.EveryAdvantage.net.

Below are 16 rectangles of four different shades. As you can see, there are 4 rectangles of each shade, and they are in no particular order.

Your first assignment is to visualize, in your mind only, what it would look like if the rectangles were organized in the "right" order. Think about that for a second and then try to organize the rectangles in your mind.

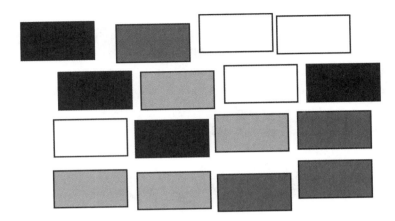

Now the first thing you may ask is, "How can I organize something in my mind if I don't even know what it's supposed to look like!" If that's the case, congratulations! You got the first point, which is that it helps to know what something is supposed to look like before you put a plan together to achieve it. In fact it's almost impossible to create a plan for anything if you don't have a clear idea of what the end outcome is supposed to "look" like.

It may also occur to you that it would be a lot easier to organize the rectangles if you could cut them out and move them around a bit, say, on a table. That would help you create a clearer idea of what the various design possibilities are more quickly than you would if you had to do it all in your head. You'd simply be better organized.

If you agree with that statement, congrats again! You've gotten the second point. Putting something down in front of you so you can look at and make changes or adjustments on the spot is a whole lot easier to work with than if you try to do all the work in your head.

Even the most gifted of artists will often draft a sketch of what they want to paint or sculpt before they start the actual work. It simply helps them to have a visual guide to help them execute the clear "vision" of what they are thinking.

Okay. Suppose I said that if you go to page 210 in your *Making Connections: Plug-It-In and Work-It-Out Tool Kit*, you'll see a picture of what the "right" configuration of the pieces is supposed to look like. By the way the correct design, in this case, is the design in the middle. Does seeing the right design help you organize the pieces any better? Of course it would. If you know what the end result is supposed to be, or supposed to look like, it becomes much easier to organize things and achieve them more quickly.

Think about putting together a jigsaw puzzle. Could you put the puzzle together faster if you had the picture of the finished puzzle on the lid of the box, or would it be easier to put together if you had no idea at all what the puzzle was supposed to look like? You know the answer.

If you'd like to play with this concept a bit more, go to www.EveryAdvantage.net and print out two copies of "Solving Life's Puzles." Cut one of them into the 16 rectangular pieces. Get a watch with a second hand and ask a friend to organize the puzzle correctly without giving her a copy of the correctly completed design. Give her 30 seconds to get it right.

Next, time her again, but this time show her what the design is supposed to look like. I'm sure you'll find that literally everyone will put the puzzle together faster when they have a clear picture of the desired outcome, just as you will find it easier to accomplish your personal goals once you write out exactly what they are.

So here's a summary of what we just covered. First, you are more likely to achieve any goal if you have a clear and specific picture of what that goal is. Second, you will find it easier to achieve your goals when they are written down, because doing so will help you crystallize what you want to achieve. Just keeping the goal in your mind will not create a clear picture for you.

So make sure that you set clear personal goals and that you put them down in writing. Both will be important to helping you accomplish the things you want.

Enough Inches Do Make a Foot

Okay. Let's look at goal setting in the context of a story.

Three young children were out at the beach early one morning. The beach had just been "combed" the night before and was smooth and clean. Seeing the wide open space, one of the children decided to challenge the others to a contest. The challenge was to see which of the three kids could cross the beach and make the straightest line in the sand. The others accepted the challenge and they began.

The beach was roughly 100 yards across from the parking lot to the water with a playground, volleyball court, lifeguard station, some palm trees, and a lot of trash cans, just like a lot of other beaches.

The first child, a little boy in a blue swimsuit, began walking across the beach toward the water. Not really having much of a plan, he just kept walking, looking forward and assuming he was headed in a straight line. "After all," he thought, "how hard can it be to walk a straight line and get to the other side of the beach?"

The little boy didn't have any particular place in mind he wanted to end up except to get to the other side of the beach. He figured that if he just headed there, the line he walked would naturally be straight. But not only was his path not straight, about 20 yards before he would have arrived at the water, the young boy decided to chase away a flock of seagulls that had gathered on the beach. Turns out he got a little distracted and forgot about the objective of his walk.

So, needless to say, not only did the little boy not make a straight line in the sand, he never made it all the way across the beach.

The second child, a little girl in a red, polka-dotted one-piece, paused for a moment. "I see why he didn't walk in a straight line," she said to herself. "He didn't even turn around once to see if his line was straight. Surely if I just keep an eye on where I've walked, focus on where I've been, I can walk a straight line across the beach," she thought.

So, with that logic, the little girl walked across the beach facing backwards so she could keep an eye on her path as she walked. If she would look back, she surmised, she'd be able to keep an eye on her path at all times.

The little girl began to walk backwards across the beach. After taking a few steps, she noticed that her line wasn't exactly straight, and she immediately corrected her path. She took a brief glimpse to the other side of the beach and again noticed that she was not going to end up where she had intended, so again she adjusted her direction. She did this several times until she arrived at the edge of the water. When she looked at her path after she'd finished, it was obvious that she had overcorrected her path several times and ended up walking in a zigzag pattern. This was partially caused by the fact that she wasn't sure whether to look forward or look back, and her path reflected her confusion.

The third child, another little girl in a green bathing suit, noticed what the other two children had done. She recognized that the first child tried to walk across the beach in one continuous path and wasn't successful. She also noticed that the second child walked across the beach in a series of smaller paths, but because she focused only on where she was coming from and didn't see where she was going, she repeatedly went out of her way and had to correct her path many times.

The little girl in the green bathing suit realized that in order to walk across the beach in a straight line, she'd have to carve up her trip into a number of smaller lines, while looking forward, because she could easily walk a straight line that was short. She also knew that if she could walk in a series of shorter, straight lines, she would ensure that her final path was straight.

To accomplish this, the little girl looked across the beach for landmarks she could use to help guide her. After examining the situation, she noticed that there were several landmarks, including a couple of trash cans, the volleyball court, and a park bench all lined up in a straight line going all the way across the beach. She knew that if she could walk from one landmark to another, her path would end up being straight.

So she started her journey with her eye focused on each of the landmarks. She started at the bench and walked to the first trash can, then to the volleyball court, and then to the other trash can, to the park bench, and finally to the water's edge. To no one's surprise, the third child walked an almost perfectly straight line across the beach and won the contest.

The Result

So what exactly happened here? Why did the first two children end up so far off their intended mission while the third child was dead on?

The first child initially had his mind on one thing—getting to the other side of the beach. He was concerned with the final outcome, but it was 100 yards away. He started by walking in what he thought was the right direction, but he had no plan to make the path straight and subsequently lost focus and got distracted by the seagulls gathered nearby.

The little boy didn't have a plan to make a straight path. He didn't see any need to plan anything since he "knew" he would eventually end up on the other side of the beach anyway—that is, until he became distracted by the squawking gulls.

So much for looking only at the end result when he should also have considered how to get there.

The second child, who thought she knew better, spent quite a bit of time looking back on the path she had already walked. She thought that concentrating on what she had done already would give her a better perspective on how she might walk a straight path. Though looking back did give her some clues that she was not walking the intended straight line, it became increasingly more difficult to straighten the line as she continuously corrected her path by looking backward. She thought that she could get to her destination by focusing on her past accomplishments. It obviously didn't work.

The little girl in the green swimsuit had it figured out. She knew that making a straight line across a 100-yard beach would be very difficult if she looked at it as a single objective. Instead she figured out that she could create a series of shorter straight lines that would be easier to accomplish and in the end would create the single straight line—the desired outcome.

So what can we learn from this story? The answer is:

1) You must know something about what you want your life and your goals to look like.
2) If a goal is too far away, you may get distracted from achieving it.
3) Dwelling on the past and expecting your previous accomplishments to get you to your goal is not a dependable strategy.
4) It can be a lot easier to achieve a big goal if you break it down into a series of smaller goals.
5) Even if you understand what you want to achieve, you need to have a plan to achieve it.

That's the Way It Works

If you try to achieve your goals like the first child did, you may lose sight of the ultimate outcome and stray from the right way of achieving it. There are often many details or distractions on the way to achieving a goal, so it's quite easy to get side-tracked on your journey. Put another way, anyone can have a dream for his or her life, but you need to have a plan to achieve it.

From another perspective, when someone focuses only on the ultimate outcome, the goal can seem very large and overwhelming—so overwhelming, in fact, that he or she just gives up trying. Have you ever given up on something because it seemed overwhelming?

All you need to do to ensure that you are able to achieve your goals in a manageable way is to create a plan of shorter, interim steps, or subgoals. By doing that, you'll ultimately achieve your end goal. Your natural sense of perseverance will enable you to see the light at the end of each short tunnel. That will help you feel like you're making progress, and you'll be more likely to keep going until you achieve your ultimate goal.

If you try to achieve your goals the way the second child did, you won't be focused on what you need to do but rather on what you have already done. Goal achievement results from a series of steps forward and from looking at what needs to be done next. Although the past does offer some valuable lessons, people who concentrate only on the past will find it difficult to move in a positive way into the future. Do you know anyone who dwells on the past?

Now let's move ahead and learn the core principles of personal goal setting. You'll also learn how to make goal setting work for you so you can achieve the highest levels of success and personal fulfillment in anything you do.

Adopt the goal setting principles we'll cover here, and you will find yourself achieving things you may never have thought possible.

Your Personal Goal Setting Plan

We've established that having personal goals will help you reach the success you want sooner and easier, so it's time to learn how to set goals that work.

A good place to start is to define the types of goals you will set at one time or another. There are essentially 6 areas of life for which you'll set personal goals. Those are:

- ◆ **Home Life:** Goals related to family, home, where you live, etc.

- ◆ **Economic:** Goals related to financial issues and career.

- ◆ **Social:** Goals related to your social life, friends, cultural issues, etc.

- ◆ **Spiritual:** Goals related to religion, moral and ethical issues.

- ◆ **Physical:** Goals involving health and physical well-being.

- ◆ **Mental:** Goals related to education, learning, and mental growth.

It's important to set personal goals in all areas of life that have value to you. If you concentrate on goal setting in only one area of life, you may well achieve those goals. However the price you'll pay will be an unbalanced life and that has its consequences.

Imagine focusing only on your career. What would be likely to happen if the other areas of your life don't get the proper amount of attention?

What if you focused only on physically working out? Would you be likely to excel in other areas as well? Or think about what would happen if you planned your whole life exclusively around your social activities? Would other areas likely suffer? I think you'll agree that the answer is "yes." The road in life can become quite bumpy if you decide to ignore setting goals for areas of life that have important value to you. Balance is the key.

Think about it this way. Pick one area of life in which you could care less if you ever achieve anything. Perhaps you would be okay ignoring your family and your home life. Maybe you have no interest in the financial or career area. Or maybe you don't care about having a social life. Perhaps you are not a spiritual person and could care less about being ethical and moral. Or perhaps you'd be okay with letting your health fall apart. And finally you may not give a hoot about learning anything or challenging yourself mentally.

Now if you are like most people, you'd probably say, "Hold on a minute. Each of those areas has some level of importance to me." If that is the case, you can see why it is important to have personal goals set for each area of life.

I don't want to confuse the need to have a balanced life with the understanding that there will be tradeoffs. We each have a limited amount of time to accomplish everything we want to. That's why it's so important for us to understand our personal values. By understanding our personal values, it becomes easier to allocate the right amount of time to the areas of life we most value.

Remember, without having personal goals, you won't have a clear direction to move toward consciously. And if you don't have a defined direction for one or more areas of life, the only way you'll ever get anywhere is by accident.

In this chapter you'll learn how to select and structure your wants to design effective goals you can pursue and achieve with energy and enthusiasm. So let's get started on defining your personal goals for success!

Please go to page 211 in *your Making Connections: Plug-It-In and Work-It-Out Tool Kit,* or log onto www.EveryAdvantage.net, and you'll find a tool called "Everything I Want to Have and Do."

This tool will help you start to define what your personal goals might be. First list all the things you want or think you want for each area of life. From there you'll zero in on the areas you most want to concentrate on and achieve. (By the way, don't expect to complete your list of everything you want right now because your list will change and grow over time.) For now begin your list with as many things as you can think of. Don't be concerned right now with whether they seem achievable. Just list everything you could possibly want to have or to do.

When you're ready, come back here and you'll learn more about how to set effective goals.

Establishing Effective Goals

How did it feel to write down a list of everything you'd ever want to have or to achieve? Was it easy or difficult? Were there certain areas of life for which you found it easier to list things? Were there areas you found more difficult? Is it clear to you now which things are the most important to you? No? If not, don't worry. If you're like most people, you're not quite there yet.

You just finished (actually started) listing a ton of things you'd like to have or do, but how many of those things are important enough to you that you will actually pursue them? Chances are that there are only a handful of wants you will consider important enough for you to take the time and resources to pursue seriously.

An attainable goal must be something you want to achieve and are willing to work toward achieving. A simple want, or a wish, is something you'd like to do or have. You undoubtedly have several of those on your list. But a simple want or wish may be something you wouldn't necessarily be willing to commit the time, energy, or resources to get. Wishes are nice ideas and thoughts whereas goals are the things you are serious about going for.

For instance on my original list of things I want I included earning a black belt in a martial art. Aikido was the one I had in mind. I like the idea of being a black belt and would love to have the skills of one. However, I don't think, at least at this point in my life, that I could commit the time to take classes, study, and practice. Therefore I would not see earning a black belt in a martial art as a goal of mine today. I like the idea, the concept, but I wouldn't be able to put the goal into action. So for now I'll leave it as a want . . . a goal-in-waiting if you will . . . and when I'm ready to pursue the black belt, I'll structure my want as a goal.

Put on Your *S.M.A.R.T. C.A.P.*

An effective goal has a very distinct structure to it. Unless all elements of the structure are in place, it really won't be as effective a goal. It may simply look more like a want or a desire. Like any structure, a goal has specific parts it needs to make it strong.

Just like a house needs a roof, a floor, walls, bathrooms, a kitchen, and so on to be useful, there are certain elements of a goal that must be in place in order for the goal to be as useful as possible . . . in order for it to work right.

Let's look at those specific elements, or parts, now.

A quality goal must pass what I call the *S.M.A.R.T. C.A.P.* test. In other words it must be Specific, Measurable, Attainable, Relevant, and Time bound. In addition an effective goal should have a Cost component, include an Action verb, and be stated in a Positive way.

Let's walk through each of these characteristics so you can see why each is needed. We'll start with the essential components of a SMART goal and put the "CAP" on in a minute.

Specific

First a goal must be specific rather than vague. That's because your brain can focus on something that is specific, and it can't focus on something that is not. If you say the words "a lot," your brain won't get a crystal-clear picture the way it would if you said "1,000."

There's a big difference between saying, "My goal is to spend more time with my friends" and "My goal is to go to the art museum this Saturday for two hours with Sam and Debbie."

Think about it. What does spending more time with your friends mean? Doing what? When specifically? Which friends? How much is "more"?

When you write down the specifics of your goal, your brain can then focus on helping you achieve the exact results you want, because it can see the picture you are trying to achieve.

Knowing specifically what outcome you are seeking will help your mind start to work out the details to get you to that outcome (remember that we've talked about how the mind focuses on the picture you create). But without specific details, the brain has little if anything to focus on. And if it can't focus on a specific outcome, it can't help guide you to achieve one.

If you say you want to be a success, your brain doesn't know exactly what "success" looks like unless you form a mental picture of it. But if you say something like, "I'd like to own a new Honda® Civic automobile," your brain can focus on the particular car you want.

Measurable

Next your goal should be measurable. That simply means that you will be able to tell if you achieve the goal or not. For example, let's say that your goal is to become financially well off. What exactly is the definition of "financially well off" and how will you know if you achieve your goal? The definition of "financially well off" is not the issue. Rather give your goal a specific measurement that, when met, tells you that you have achieved your objective.

How about saying, "I'd like to accumulate a personal net worth of $5,000,000 by the time I am 35"? The clear measurement is achieving the number of $5,000,000. You either achieve it or you don't. More importantly having a measurable outcome gives your mind specific details for you to shoot for. Without the measurable details how will you know if you actually are financially well off? With specific measurements in place your mind can begin to go to work helping you achieve very concrete outcomes.

Another example would be to say, "I'd like to score at least 200 points in a game of bowling this week." That statement is a lot more measurable than saying, "I want to bowl a good game." Your mind can't focus on the abstract idea of "a good game," but it sure can tell what 200 points looks like.

Attainable

An attainable goal simply means that the goal is possible to achieve, but it should also require you to go beyond simply going through the daily motions of life to achieve it. Obviously a goal needs to be possible to achieve or it shouldn't even be considered a goal. It would simply be a pie in the sky wish if it were impossible.

In the example I gave earlier, achieving a black belt in a martial art is not attainable for me at this time. I've simply got too many other things going on to study for a black belt. And since it is not truly attainable for me now given other priorities, I have not made it a goal. It is still a "want" but not a goal.

An important part of being attainable is that the goal should also be challenging. Something that is easily attainable and not challenging is probably not worthwhile to set as a goal. Why is that? Because if the goal isn't challenging, it is human nature to lose interest in it. If something is attainable but not challenging, it is nothing more than an errand.

Let's look a little closer at why you want your goals to have some challenge to them.

Suppose you had a bunch of ping-pong balls and an empty bucket. If I place the bucket immediately in front of you and tell you to try to get 100 ping-pong balls in the bucket, one at a time, how long would that keep your interest? Not very long, I presume. Your brain would quickly be saying to you, "Man, is this lame. There's no challenge."

And what if I took the bucket and moved it 50 feet away from you and asked you to throw the 100 ping-pong balls into the bucket? How long would that keep you interested? Again, not very long I'll bet. This time not because it was overly easy, boring, and redundant, but because the odds of your throwing even a single ping-pong ball into a bucket 50 feet away is pretty darn slim, much less 100 of them. In this case your mind will say, "Give it up already. It's not worth trying."

So the ideal level for a goal is one that is attainable yet challenging. In this situation, attainable yet challenging might mean putting the bucket 10 feet in front of you—just far enough to make it a challenge, but not so far away as to make the goal impossible. Because it is attainable yet challenging, you would find this game more enjoyable than the versions that were too easy or too difficult. The challenge would hold your attention, and if you want to achieve any goal, the challenge of the goal will need to hold your attention.

Relevant

Personal goals need to be relevant to you.

First a personal goal must have purpose and be meaningful to you. A goal is irrelevant if it is someone else's goal. In order to be relevant, a goal must be yours.

Say you set a goal to become a U.S. Air Force officer because that is what your dad wants you to be, but your real interest is to be an actor. The goal to become an Air Force officer wouldn't be a personal goal of yours, because it is not your goal but rather your dad's. It is not relevant to you.

A goal is not relevant to you unless you personally see meaning and purpose to it. If the goal is not relevant to you and what you want, then it is not worth setting as a goal of yours.

In the same way each subgoal must support the end goal for it to be relevant. For example if you have a goal to get into a prestigious university, a supporting goal that says, "I will get at least all C's and D's in high school and will graduate in at least the top three-quarters of my class" does not match up with your desire to get into a top school. Earning C's and D's is irrelevant to that goal because the goal is set too low and will be of no help in getting you into the school you want.

To say you will shoot for A's and B's, on the other hand, would be a far more relevant subgoal to help achieve your end goal.

Time Bound

The last element of a SMART goal is that is must be time bound. In other words it must have a deadline for achieving it. Without a deadline the goal would be open-ended and lack the sense of urgency needed to achieve it.

To say that you want to graduate from college may sound like a complete goal, but it isn't unless it has a time component attached to it.

When do you want to graduate from college? By the time you are 22 years old? 25? 35? 65? Without making the goal time bound, all you have is a concept, not a goal. In essence, the time component of your goal is another way in which you can hold yourself accountable and measure your success.

Cost Component

In addition to the SMART components, the most effective goals are also "capped" off with these details. Each of these CAP components will help ensure that the structure of your goal supports your efforts.

A successful goal should have a cost component. That means that your goal must state what you will do to achieve the goal and the price you will pay to achieve it. The cost component of the goal is what you will give up, or invest, in order to achieve the goal. That may be time, money, or other resources. To achieve any goal, there is always something you will need to give up to do so.

So, for example, to say, "My goal is to be the best golfer in the state" may sound like a good goal, but it doesn't tell the whole story. It doesn't hold you to anything that tells what price you will pay to achieve the goal—what you will have to do or give up to attain the goal. To gain anything in life, you must trade it for something. This is a natural law.

Instead the goal might better read as, "My goal is to be the best golfer in the state, and I will achieve my goal by practicing at least four hours each week." Now the goal has some meat to it. You can better manage the goal now since you know what you will have to commit (what the cost will be) to achieve it, namely four hours of your time each week. The cost component helps you clarify the discipline you will need to demonstrate in order to achieve the goal, and you'll always have something to consider that will tell you whether you have invested a resource to achieve the goal or not.

Action Verb

A quality goal has an action verb in it that says specifically what action you will take to achieve the goal. In the example above the action verb is "practice." Or your goal might be, "I will accumulate a net worth of $1,000,000 by the time I am 30 years old by investing in real estate." The action verb here is "investing" as it describes the action you will take to achieve the goal. Imagine the same goal stated without the action verb. The statement would then simply be only half of the equation. It would say what you want to achieve, but it wouldn't say how you would do it. Your mind needs to know how you plan on doing something so it can help you take the right action.

Positively Stated

Finally, a quality goal must be stated positively as opposed to negatively. The goal must state what you will do or will achieve rather than what you won't do. That's because the human mind tends to focus on the mental picture you give it. So if your goal is to "Stop eating sweets beginning this month," your mind sees the mental image of "eating sweets." It cannot see the act of "not eating." There is no way to create a mental picture of not eating, because to think of not eating, you must also consider what it is you are not doing, namely eating.

Instead you might state this goal by saying, "Beginning today, I will eat only healthy foods." This version of the goal sets the mental picture of your eating healthy foods, so the picture in your mind focuses on what you think of as healthy foods. Your mind will give you a clearer image of what you will eat as opposed to what you should avoid.

The negatively stated goal uses the verbiage "eating sweets," which is the mental picture your mind will construct into reality for you. You will be more successful in setting and achieving your goals if you tell your mind what you do want it to focus on, as opposed to what it shouldn't.

Think about it. If I say to you, "Stop thinking about eating sweets," what does your mind immediately picture? I'm sure you had to form a mental image of sweets, simply because of the way I phrased the statement. The exact same thing applies to the goals you set.

Here's another example. Your goal is not to think of a pink giraffe. Ready? Go! Did you think of a pink giraffe? Yes, you did, because the statement was structured in a way that called out what you wanted to avoid, namely thinking of a pink giraffe.

Finally don't look at what's at the bottom of this page. Hey, get your eyes back here. I said don't look.

See what I mean?

Show Me How It Works

We've now covered each of the *S.M.A.R.T. C.A.P.* characteristics of a highly effective goal. To end this topic I'll give you a couple of examples of *S.M.A.R.T. C.A.P.* goals so you'll have models to work from.

1. "Beginning the day after New Year's Day, I will set aside at least $3.00 each week to buy my family their holiday gifts next year."

- Is it specific? Yep. It says exactly what you will do.

- Measurable? Again yes. Three dollars a week is a measurable characteristic.

- Attainable? Seems to be. Three dollars a week is not a lot to ask.

- Relevant? Yes, if being able to afford holiday gifts is something you want to accomplish.

- Time bound? Uh huh. In fact, you have two time goals here. The first is to have enough money to buy gifts by holiday time. The other is actually 50 or so weekly deadlines to put aside $3 each week.

- Does it have a cost component? Yes. Setting aside money is inherently a cost component, as you are giving up the opportunity to use that money elsewhere.

- Action verb? Yes, "set aside" is an action of doing something.

- Is it stated in the positive? Again yes. It describes what you will do as opposed to what you won't do. No negative words such as "stop," "don't," "avoid," and so on are in the goal.

Here's another one.

2. "I will develop a six-pack of abs by May 30 by taking 5 minutes each day to complete at least 100 sit-ups."

- Is it specific?—Yes. It says exactly what you will do, 100 sit-ups every day.

- Measurable? Again yes. A hundred sit-ups a day is a measurable characteristic.

- ◆ Attainable? Seems to be. A hundred sit-ups a day takes only a couple of minutes to do.

- ◆ Relevant? Yes, if looking buff is something that is important to you.

- ◆ Time bound? Yes. Again you have two deadlines. First to develop a six-pack by May 30 and secondly you have daily deadlines to do 100 sit-ups each day.

- ◆ Does it have a cost component? Yes. In this case you'll use 5 minutes each day.

- ◆ Action verb? Yes. The word *complete*.

- ◆ Is it stated in the positive? Again yes. It describes what you will do as opposed to what you won't do. No negative words such as "stop," "don't," "avoid," and so on are in the goal.

As you can see, constructing *S.M.A.R.T. C.A.P.* goals is actually quite easy. It may have taken me a few pages to explain the concept to you, but it will take only a moment to write an effective goal in *S.M.A.R.T. C.A.P.* form.

Put Your Goals in Writing

The final important thing about developing effective goals is that you should put them in writing. The *FlashPoint* goal planning tool called "My Personal Goal Plan" is on page 219 in your *Making Connections: Plug-It-In and Work-It-Out Tool Kit*. You may want to take a quick look at it to familiarize yourself with the tool.

You might ask, "Why should I bother writing down a goal? Isn't it enough that I just know what the goal is?"

There are a number of reasons for putting your goals in writing.

1. When you write down your goals, you are simultaneously

recording them mentally, visually, and tactilely (through touch). When all of these senses are used, your mind begins to create a more concrete reality of the goal.

2. Your mind begins to work on how to structure the goal correctly, because you are forced to think about specifics of the goal when you write it down in *S.M.A.R.T. C.A.P.* form.

3. Your mind also starts to work on accomplishing the goal when you physically record it, because it can see what needs to be accomplished and the plan to accomplish it. You've begun to lay out a mental roadmap for the goal's attainment.

4. When you physically write down a goal, you begin to commit mentally that the goal is something you will pursue. It's the difference between thinking about doing something and taking the first step toward doing it. When you put a goal in writing, you've told your subconscious that the goal is important enough to write down, so your subconscious starts to work on helping you achieve it.

5. You'll have a reference you can come back to over and over. As you expand your list of personal goals, recording your goals in writing will keep track of them for you and create a big "to do" list you can refer to often.

6. Writing out your goals will keep you organized and focused. You'll be more likely to stay on target instead of getting distracted by other things that pop up.

So write down your goals if you are serious about achieving them. You probably wouldn't go to the grocery store without a list of items to buy because out of sight, out of mind, as they say. So why would you try to go through something as important as your life without a list of your personal goals you can refer to?

Subgoals

For each personal goal you set for yourself, you'll probably use a series of subgoals that will lead you to accomplish your end goal. Like the child whose goal was to walk a straight line across the sandy beach and who lined up several subgoals (i.e., walking straight lines between each of the trash cans, the volley-ball court, and the bench), you will be able to identify subgoals to help you achieve your end goals.

Subgoals can be effectively determined by simply looking at your end goal and tracing back each step you would have to take to get there. Police departments use a similar technique to determine how a crime was committed. They start from the scene of the crime (the end result) and build a sequence of events backward until they find the suspect.

Let's take an example. We already looked at how subgoals work in sequence when we talked about a pro football team. There was a series of subgoals the football team needed to accomplish to earn a Super Bowl ring.

Now let's take an example of a subgoal strategy that may be a bit more practical. Say you wanted to become a doctor. What subgoals might you have to accomplish along the way to achieve that end goal? To find the answers, let's trace the subgoals backward.

- ◆ Before you can become a doctor, you must graduate from medical school.

- ◆ To graduate from med school, you would first need to be accepted to one.

- ◆ In order to be accepted to med school, you'd have to score well on the MCAT, the standard medical school admissions test.

- ◆ You'd also need to score in the top 5-10% of your class in your undergraduate studies.

- ◆ Getting good grades in your pre-med science courses alone would also be an important goal.

- ◆ To get good grades in college, you would most likely need to spend several hours a day studying.

- ◆ Just to get into your undergrad university, you would need to graduate high school with a respectable GPA.

- ◆ And so on.

So subgoals are really nothing more than the stepping stones you must cross to achieve your end goal.

The setting of subgoals is the component of goal setting that makes attaining your end goals more manageable. Rather than being overwhelmed with the end goal itself, your subgoals break down the end goal into smaller, manageable goals that progressively get you closer to achieving your end goal.

Remember, each subgoal should also meet the *S.M.A.R.T. C.A.P.* test or they are just tasks.

Crystallizing Your Goals

You now know how to write effective goals. You also started a list of everything you want to have or achieve. Our next step will be to help you identify and write a limited list of goals you are most likely to pursue and achieve in the short term. Why the short term?

The most effective way to start your personal goal setting plan is to select one or two shorter-range goals you can accomplish in the near future, say in 90 days or less. We'll begin with these short-term goals, because it will be helpful to you to enjoy quickly the satisfaction of achieving them. Once you feel the success of setting, acting on, and achieving goals you've planned, you'll increase your confidence in your ability to achieve any goal you set your mind to.

If you think about what I just said, you'll realize that we're making personal goal setting a goal itself! We're starting with a shorter, more attainable subgoal (attainably challenging) that will lead you closer to, and more comfortable with, the end goal—which should be to make personal goal setting a permanent part of your life.

"Why" or "W.I.F.M."

Now that we've discussed in detail how to set goals and the process for making progress on your goals, it's time to learn something that will make or break your ability to achieve your goals, namely, how to choose personal goals you will strive for with passion.

Remember, there is a difference between a mere "want" and a "goal." A want simply takes imagination, but a goal requires something much stronger. To achieve a goal requires personal commitment.

So what is it that makes a goal something you'll be passionately committed to and motivated to achieve?

To identify goals that are the most important to you, you must clearly understand exactly why you want to achieve each respective goal (sound like something we've already covered?). To come up with that answer, simply ask yourself, "What's in it for me?" —or W.I.I.F.M, for short. You need to know the reasons that will drive you to achieve your goal, because the why behind the goal is the most powerful factor in determining whether you'll achieve your goal or not.

The W.I.I.F.M. behind the goal is your motivation, your reason for wanting to achieve it. So to identify a goal that has staying power, you first need to think about the reasons why you want to achieve a particular goal. Only when the "why" behind achieving your goal is strong enough will you be likely to do "what" it takes to achieve the goal.

Having strong reasons for achieving your goal will help you plow right through any distractions or roadblocks that could derail your efforts to achieve it. And the stronger the reasons you have for wanting to achieve the goal, the more likely you will.

Think about the people you know who have achieved at any level. Behind each and every one of their achievements you'll find a strong personal reason for their achieving it. The bottom line is that people won't try to achieve things that are not important to them. But when something becomes important, it has meaning to it. It has a strong reason behind your wanting to achieve it. The stronger the reasons, the more dedicated your drive will be to achieve the goal. So understand your reasons behind the goal, the W.I.I.F.M., and you'll have great insight as to whether those reasons are strong enough to take you to the finish line.

You'll soon be using the "My Personal Goal Plan" tool I referred to earlier to help you crystallize your goals and your plans for achieving them. There is a section on this tool that asks for your reasons (the "whys") for wanting to achieve each of your goals.

This section of each goal plan will be very valuable to you. It will help you decide whether the goal is worth pursuing. Then, later on, it will give you something to come back to and remind you of exactly why you set the goal in the first place. Sometimes you'll find that simple reminder really helpful in giving you a kick in the pants and getting you back on track to achieving your goal. This will be particularly helpful in "down" moments, as it will help rebuild your motivation and understanding regarding the importance of the goal to you.

I'd like to leave this section with a quote from Dr. Dennis Waitley, one of the foremost authorities on personal development. In his work, *The New Dynamics of Goal Setting,* he said, "We spend too much time and energy worrying about the things we want to do but can't instead of concentrating on the things we can do but don't."

Take Dr. Waitley's advice: identify those goals you can and want to do something about, and get on with it.

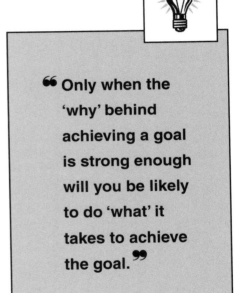

❝ Only when the 'why' behind achieving a goal is strong enough will you be likely to do 'what' it takes to achieve the goal. ❞

Celebrate Your Success!

Finally, celebrate your success. That means that whenever you achieve a goal, or even a subgoal, do something special for yourself. After all you earned it. Rewarding yourself in this way will do a couple of things for you.

First it will make you feel even better about your accomplishment since you are telling yourself that the accomplishment is worthy of celebration.

Secondly, when you reward yourself for an achievement, you are giving your subconscious another reason to help you achieve even more goals. You will begin to condition your subconscious to understand that you will be rewarded when a goal is achieved, and it will therefore work that much harder to help you achieve more goals.

So celebrate your successes. You are worth it.

Action Item!

The easiest way to get into the rhythm of personal goal setting is to begin by writing down simple tasks you want to accomplish the next day on a 3"x5" card or enter them into your PDA (personal digital assistant) if you have one. This can be done right before going to sleep or right after you wake up in the morning. You can write down one thing or several things, and the items needn't be complicated. The task could be something as easy as "Call Pat by 3:00 pm" or "Work out before dinner."

There are a couple of reasons for doing this prior to starting your broader goal setting program. First it will get you in the habit of writing down what you want to accomplish. (Remember, writing down your goals is critical to achieving them.) Secondly, since most of the things you'll list on your 3"x5" cards or PDA will be easily achievable and you will complete them the next day, it will teach your mind that you can set and achieve goals.

Once you start writing down what you want to achieve and believe you can achieve the goals you write down, you're half-way to achieving any goal you want.

After you've done this for several days (preferably for two weeks or so to really condition yourself), you'll be ready to begin using the "My Personal Goal Plan" tool in the book, or you can get a larger 8.5"x11"" version at www.EveryAdvantage.net. Remember you can make additional copies of this tool, or of any tool we've discussed, right from the Website.

"My Personal Goal Plan" is designed to help you structure your goals in the right way as well as to help you determine any obstacles you may have to overcome in order to achieve your goals.

On the top of the page on "My Personal Goal Plan" you'll see a box that asks for which area of life you want to work on your goals.

Use your list of "Everything I Want to Have and Do" for that particular area of life to help you decide where you want to start.

As we discussed earlier, in the blank with the heading "Term," you'd put an "S" if the goal is a short-term goal, an "M" if it is a medium-term goal, or an "L" if the goal would take more than one year to complete.

You'll also see a space under the heading "Importance" next to each item you listed on "Everything I Want to Have and Do." If you haven't already done so, on that space put a number "1" next to any goal that is particularly important to you and that you feel you are ready to begin working on.

Next rewrite each of the "wants" you plan to start treating as a goal in *S.M.A.R.T C.A.P.* form on a separate "My Goal Plan" form. Then complete the "My Goal Plan" form for each short-term goal in each goal category and begin pursuing those goals according to the plan you lay out.

Feel free to go back and refer to any sections of *FlashPoint* as a refresher.

Review

1. Without personal goals how will you know where it is you want to go, and how will you know if you get there? You literally can't "score" a goal in life unless you know exactly what the goal is.
2. In the simplest terms a true "goal" is a specific outcome that you are committed to achieving and willing to support with a plan and action.
3. Without knowing what you are aiming for, without defining the outcome you are working toward, how will you know if you ever achieve anything worthwhile? If you don't have a defined place to go, a defined outcome, how will you know when or if you get there? You won't, because there is no "there" to get to.
4. Not having clearly defined goals is one of the most common characteristics of those who don't achieve much in life.
5. Your goal plan is your reference point that you can go back to over and over not only to remind you of what you want, but also to help you keep a clear picture in your mind of what you are trying to accomplish.
6. All you need to do to ensure that you are able to achieve your goals in a manageable way is to create a plan of

shorter, interim steps or subgoals that will ultimately lead you to achieving your end goal.

7. Types of goals:

- ◆ Home Life: Goals related to family, home, where you live, etc.
- ◆ Economic: Goals related to financial issues and career.
- ◆ Social: Goals related to your social life, friends, cultural issues, etc.
- ◆ Spiritual: Goals related to religion, moral and ethical issues.
- ◆ Physical: Goals involving health and physical well-being.
- ◆ Mental: Goals related to education, learning, and mental growth.

8. A quality goal must pass the *S.M.A.R.T. C.A.P.* test:

- ◆ Specific
- ◆ Measurable
- ◆ Attainably challenging
- ◆ Relevant
- ◆ Time bound
- ◆ Cost component
- ◆ Action verb
- ◆ Positively stated

9. Put your goals in writing.
10. The why or W.I.I.F.M. behind the goal is the most powerful indicator as to whether you'll achieve your goal or not. Only when the "why" behind achieving a goal is strong enough will you be likely to do what it takes to achieve the goal.

Bringing It All Together

Congratulations on Completing
FlashPoint: Ignite Your Potential!

W e've covered a lot of ground together, and you've taken a huge step toward improving your ability to have the successes you want in life. You did that by creating a better understanding of yourself and the world around you, and I'm confident you'll find doing so a big advantage in helping you get to where you want, and what you want, faster.

We looked at the four stages of learning and that learning is a process that can take time. So in order to get good at anything, you may have to do it a number of times to master it. I encourage you to hang in there and keep that thought in mind as you continue your journey in life.

You learned about the importance of personal awareness and that in order to take conscious action on anything, whether it is a task, a goal, changing a behavior, or whatever, you must first be aware of the thing you want to act on.

I introduced the concept of a *FlashPoint* to you . . . the point at which you realize something you may not have before and then take conscious action to use the newly discovered insight. At the same time we discussed that even the best knowledge is only a potential source of power waiting to be used. In order to convert that knowledge to power and get what you want, you have to use that knowledge through action.

Next we covered the concepts of success and failure. We determined that success is a process and not merely a destination. It is the process of doing the right things in the right way in order to achieve a worthwhile objective. We also talked about the fact that a success is not something you become. Instead it is a condition you attract to you.

We also learned that failing is not the same thing as failure and that sometimes we need to fail in order to be successful. In other words we learn through failing.

I also offered my definition of what failure is. I defined failure as a "final attempt in life under reasonable expectations." In other words you cannot be a failure at something unless you just give up trying to achieve it.

We talked about the fear of failure and the fear of success and how they are two different ways of thinking that you will want to be aware of and manage.

Next we explored the concept of "perseverance" and how critical it is to long-term success at anything. We talked about the fact that the results you want in life may not always come immediately, but if you persevere, you can eventually achieve almost anything you put your mind to. Remember, those who succeed need take only one more step than those who fail.

We looked at the software of your life and how your personal values and beliefs directly impact everything you do or decide not to do. Your thoughts are a part of your "software" . . . part of your programming . . . and they will ultimately determine the actions you take. That's why it is so important to get in the habit of productive thinking now so you don't have to try to change a "hardened," unproductive way of thinking later. Your values and beliefs will dictate how you see life and what you do. Gaining a better understanding of your personal values and beliefs will enable you to understand why you do what you do and will give you the insights needed to change things if you want to.

In that light we determined that what your mind creates in your inner world will influence the results you get in the outer world. We learned that your mind will focus on whatever you ask it to, so you need to make sure you're asking it the right questions. We think in questions, and our mind will do everything it can to produce an answer to support the question we ask it.

We looked at some of what I refer to as "computer viruses of the mind." They included the Worry Bug (WB), the Hot Head virus (H2), and Comrade Putitoff. Next we explored some ways of overcoming those viruses.

Remember the importance of taking personal responsibility for your life. If you try to blame others for your failings, you will strip yourself of control. Don't let anybody else ever take that sense of control from you.

Finally we looked at personal goal setting and learned how to set effective goals that support our personal values and beliefs. *S.M.A.R.T. C.A.P.* was a method of creating clear and actionable goals that have all the elements needed to help you succeed in any of the 6 areas of life we looked at.

With the personal understanding you now have, you are ready to tackle a wider range of life's challenges. If you enjoyed reading *FlashPoint: Ignite Your Potential!,* I first encourage you to put what you've learned to use. I also encourage you to pick up a copy of *FlashPoint: Accelerate Your Success!,* in which you'll gain equally great insights on subjects such as living responsibly, taking risks, making good decisions, effective communication, marketing yourself, creating your personal "brand," and a whole lot about money, what it really is and how you can meet your financial goals easier.

Thanks again for reading *FlashPoint: Ignite Your Potential!* If you would like to provide me with feedback or comments on what you've read or on what you'd like to learn more about, you can contact me via email at kenolan@everyadvantage.net.

I wish you only the best!

MAKING CONNECTIONS

Plug-it-In and Work-it-Out

TOOL KIT

Number Hunt

On the following page are the numbers "1" through "60" randomly spaced in no particular order.

Your mission is to draw a continuous line from "1" to "2," from "2" to "3," from "3" to "4," and so on and to connect as many consecutive numbers as you can within 60 seconds. You'll need a stopwatch or a watch with a second hand to do this.

This same exercise is also available to print out at **www.EveryAdvantage.net** in a larger 8.5"x11" format, where a simple stop watch is provided for you.

Here's how to do the exercise. Find the number "1," on the left side of the page and then immediately start the clock and begin connecting numbers as described. Stop connecting numbers when 60 seconds is up. Go for it!

29

56 51 59

33 10

22 13 17 6

7 19 38

14 30 41 57

2 42 36 26

46 23 4 20

25 50

55 39 5

1 8 31 12 3

16 44 34 54 45

32 60 47

35 21 27

18 11 24

37 49 48 40

15 53

28 52 43 9 58

Good job. How far did you get? _____
Please go to the next page.

Okay, try it again. Start from "1" and draw a continuous line to connect the numbers in order as fast as you can. Again give yourself exactly 60 seconds.

29

56   51   59

33   10

22   13   17   6

7   19   38

14   30   41   57

2   42   36   26

46   23   4   20

25   50

55   39   5

1   8   31   12   3

16   44   34   54   45

32   60   47

35   21   27

18   11   24

37   49   48   40

15   53

28   52   43   9   58

Good job. How far did you get that time? _____
Please go to the next page.

If you're like most people, you probably got a little farther than you did the first time. If you didn't, that's okay. Some people actually do worse.

Okay, one more time. Same rules. Ready any time you are.

29
56   51   59
33   10
22   13   17   6
7   19   38
14   30   41   57
2   42   36   26
46   23   4   20
25   50
55   39   5
1   8   31   12   3
16   44   34   54   45
32   60   47
35   21   27
18   11   24
37   49   48   40
15   53
28   52   43   9   58

Great! What number did you get to? _____

Okay. You've done the same exercise three times now. List how far you got on each try on the next page.

```
First Try:        _____

Second Try:       _____

Third Try:        _____
```

Return now to page 10 to learn about what just happened and why.

My *FlashPoints* Log

Feel free to make more copies of this page, or you can print out additional full-size pages at www.EveryAdvantage.net.

Date _____

Today I realized _____

_____

I will use this FlashPoint to _____

_____

Date _____

Today I realized _____

_____

I will use this FlashPoint to _____

_____

Date _____

Today I realized _____

_____

I will use this FlashPoint to _____

_____

Date _____

Today I realized _____

_____

I will use this FlashPoint to _____

_____

Date _____

Today I realized _____

_____

I will use this FlashPoint to _____

_____

Date _____

Today I realized _____

_____

I will use this FlashPoint to _____

_____

Date _____

Today I realized _____

_____

I will use this FlashPoint to _____

_____

My Success

My Success is your tool for helping you better understand what the word "success" means to you. Having a clear definition of what the word means to *you* will help you better understand yourself and what you want to accomplish in life.

Complete each of the sentences in the spaces below. Make sure you put some thought into your answers. Don't worry if you struggle with this a bit. In fact it should be a challenging exercise for you.

You'll have another opportunity later on to come back here and redefine success based on the new things you'll have learned. It will be fascinating for you to see how your definition of success may have changed as you gained additional insights. For now, though, please complete the following exercise in pencil (because you may find yourself changing your answers later). Be as detailed or simple with your answers as you'd like. There is no right or wrong way to answer them, because your interpretation of "success" is yours and yours alone.

I define success as: _____

_____

_____

I'll know I am successful when or if: _____

_____

_____

My rules for success are: _____

_____

_____

My definition of happiness is: _____

_____

_____

My definition of personal fulfillment is: _____

_____

_____

Good job! Now let's start up where we left off on page 27 to gain some new insights into the subject of success.

Results I Want

In this exercise think about some of the areas of your life in which you don't seem to be getting the results you want. Then honestly answer the following questions about each of those areas. Examples might include:

- I'm not meeting the right people/person.
- I'm not getting the grades I want in school.
- I'm not happy with my job.
- I'm not getting enough exercise.

Here's an example of a completed exercise:

I'd like to get better results at:
    Meeting new people.

Why I think I'm not getting the results I want:
    I guess I'm just hopeful that people will introduce themselves to me. I really don't try to approach others as much as I could. I guess I'm afraid people won't like me.

What I could do differently to get better results:
    I could approach people more rather than waiting for them to come to me. Not be concerned about rejection. Create more opportunities to meet people like asking my friends to introduce me to more people they know.

When I'll start trying this new behavior:
    Friday at Angie's birthday party.

Now it's your turn. Complete as many of these statements as you'd like. Three blank formats are already provided for you here. If you'd like additional pages, you can find a full-page printable version at www.EveryAdvantage.net.

1. I'd like to get better results at: _____

_____

_____

I think I'm not getting the results I want because:

_____

_____

What I could do differently to get better results:

_____

_____

When I'll start trying this new behavior: _____

_____

_____

2. I'd like to get better results at: _____

_____

_____

I think I'm not getting the results I want because: _____

_____

_____

What I could do differently to get better results:

_____

_____

When I'll start trying this new behavior: _____

_____

_____

3. I'd like to get better results at: _____

_____

_____

I think I'm not getting the results I want because: _____

_____

_____

What I could do differently to get better results:

_____

_____

When I'll start trying this new behavior: _____

_____

_____

Feel free to make a copy of this page and keep it with you as a reminder of the new behaviors you want to try to get the results you want.

Please return now to page 36 we'll pick up where we left off.

Fear of Success Test

This questionnaire will help you determine how much or how little fear of success you may have. The result is directional only and is intended to give you a better idea of where you stand relative to fear of success.

Answer each statement honestly and we'll score it when you're finished with the exercise.

1. I generally feel guilty about being happy if a friend tells me that (s)he is depressed.

   1. Strongly Agree   2. Agree   3. Neutral   4. Disagree   5. Strongly Disagree

2. I frequently find myself not telling others about things that go well for me so they don't have to feel jealous.

   1. Strongly Agree   2. Agree   3. Neutral   4. Disagree   5. Strongly Disagree

3. I find it difficult to say "no" to people.

   1. Strongly Agree   2. Agree   3. Neutral   4. Disagree   5. Strongly Disagree

4. Before getting down to work on a project, I often suddenly find lots of other things I need to take care of first.

   1. Strongly Agree   2. Agree   3. Neutral   4. Disagree   5. Strongly Disagree

5. I tend to believe that people who look out for themselves first are selfish.

   1. Strongly Agree   2. Agree   3. Neutral   4. Disagree   5. Strongly Disagree

6. When someone I know well succeeds at something, I usually feel that I haven't done all I can to succeed.

    1. Strongly Agree   2. Agree   3. Neutral   4. Disagree   5. Strongly Disagree

7. I rarely have trouble concentrating on something for a long period of time.

    1. Strongly Disagree   2. Disagree   3. Neutral   4. Agree   5. Strongly Agree

8. When I have to ask others for their help, I feel that I'm being annoying.

    1. Strongly Agree   2. Agree   3. Neutral   4. Disagree   5. Strongly Disagree

9. I often settle with or agree with people to avoid conflict.

    1. Strongly Agree   2. Agree   3. Neutral   4. Disagree   5. Strongly Disagree

10. When I've made a decision, I'm pretty good at sticking to it.

    1. Strongly Disagree   2. Disagree   3. Neutral   4. Agree   5. Strongly Agree

11. I feel self-conscious when someone compliments me.

    1. Strongly Agree   2. Agree   3. Neutral   4. Disagree   5. Strongly Disagree

12. When I'm involved in a competitive activity (sports, a game, work), I'm often too concerned with how well I'm doing and don't enjoy the activity as much as I could.

    1. Strongly Agree   2. Agree   3. Neutral   4. Disagree   5. Strongly Disagree

13. I know I will end up disappointed if I want something too much.

    1. Strongly Disagree   2. Disagree   3. Neutral   4. Agree   5. Strongly Agree

14. Instead of wanting to celebrate, I feel let down after completing an important task or project.

    1. Strongly Agree   2. Agree   3. Neutral   4. Disagree   5. Strongly Disagree

15. For the most part I find I measure up to the standards I set for myself.

    1. Strongly Disagree   2. Disagree   3. Neutral   4. Agree   5. Strongly Agree

16. When things seem to be going really well for me, I get uneasy that I'll do something to ruin it.

    1. Strongly Agree   2. Agree   3. Neutral   4. Disagree   5. Strongly Disagree

---

Add up the numbers next to each of your responses.

Total points: _____

- If you have 56 points or more you're basically okay and not at any real risk of self-sabotaging (destructive) behavior resulting from a fear of success.

- If you have between 30 and 55 points, you're at moderate risk for self-sabotaging behavior due to some level of fear of success.

- If you have anything under 30 points, you may have a problem with a fear of success, and it's something you'll want to work on.

Please return to page 45 and we'll do a quick review of what we've learned in this chapter.

Perseverance and Commitment Enhancer

You are more likely to persevere and follow through with something if you have strong reasons *why* you want to do so. And the stronger your reasons, the more likely you are to stick with it. This tool is designed to help you identify the reasons why you want to persevere and stay committed to something. Of course, you may also discover that you don't have strong enough reasons to keep you going. In any case you can use this tool to *remind* you of the reasons you do want to persevere at something, making it all the more likely you'll achieve your objective. This same exercise is available to print out on larger pages with more writing space at www.EveryAdvantage.net.

A.

   1. I am committed to persevering at:

      _____

   2. In order to do so, I need to remind myself that:

      _____

   3. Possible reasons I may not persevere at this are:

      _____

   4. Reasons I need to persevere at this include:

      _____

B.

   1. I am committed to persevering at:

      _____

   2. In order to do so, I need to remind myself that:

      _____

   3. Possible reasons I may not persevere at this are:

      _____

   4. Reasons I need to persevere at this include:

      _____

C.

1. I am committed to persevering at:

   _____

2. In order to do so, I need to remind myself that:

   _____

3. Possible reasons I may not persevere at this are:

   _____

4. Reasons I need to persevere at this include:

   _____

D.

1. I am committed to persevering at:

   _____

2. In order to do so, I need to remind myself that:

   _____

3. Possible reasons I may not persevere at this are:

   _____

4. Reasons I need to persevere at this include:

   _____

E.

1. I am committed to persevering at:

   _____

2. In order to do so, I need to remind myself that:

   _____

3. Possible reasons I may not persevere at this are:

   _____

4. Reasons I need to persevere at this include:

   _____

If you use this tool to remind you of the things you want to follow through on, you'll soon see a difference between how committed you are to sticking with certain things and what things turn out to be less important than you originally thought. With that knowledge you can begin to build a stronger goal setting plan based on the things you feel strongest about doing. Please return now to page 57.

My Personal Values

On the following pages is a list of some of the most commonly expressed personal values. You'll use the list to gain some interesting insights about yourself. This exercise won't take long to do and will be of immeasurable value (pardon the pun) to you as you set personal goals throughout your life.

This exercise will require you to put some thought into your answers. However, most things that are worth something are not easy to come by. The important thing is that you do the exercise to learn more about yourself. Again, you can access a full page version to print out on www.EveryAdvantage.net.

Your Personal Values Inventory Exercise

Before you look at the list of values, think for a moment about what you believe your strongest personal values are. Next, go to the list and see if you can find those values listed. If you can, check off those values as "always" valued. Next, go through the list of personal values and check off how you feel about each of the other values listed. Indicate if it is something that you "always value," "often value," "sometimes value," or "rarely value." *Note: Limit your "always valued" selections to 10 values only.*

After going through this review, pay special attention to the values you rank as "always valued." These values represent your dominant values today. They are the ones you would be most likely to favor when you have to make a decision.

Once you've identified your 10 strongest values, you'll be able to determine which of those values is most dominant. Here's how you'll do it.

Start with the first of your 10 dominant values and, one by one, compare it to each of the others. Ask yourself, "Given the two values, side by side, which would I choose, most of the time, if *forced* to make a decision?"

Your most dominant values will always surface under pressure. By doing this exercise you will be able to rank your straongest personal values in order and determine which are most dominant. That's important because when you get to the chapter on goal setting, you can compare your goals to your personal values to make sure there isn't any obvious conflict that could make the goal hard to achieve. We'll talk more about that later.

Please do the exercise now. It should take about 30 minutes to complete. Here are some definitions you can use.

◆ *Always Valued* — means you consistently act according to this value. If something is always valued, it means you will always consider it when making a decision.

◆ *Often Valued* — means you usually value it, but there may be circumstances in which another value overrides it.

◆ *Sometimes Valued* — means it's something you may value given the right circumstance. It wouldn't make your short list of things you usually consider, but given the right circumstances you may consider it in your decision process.

◆ *Rarely Valued* — means just what it says. It's not something you are likely to value. The value is inconsistent with who you are and what your personal interests are.

Values	Always	Often	Sometimes	Rarely
Accomplishment/Achievement	❏	❏	❏	❏
(Knowing you've done well)				
Adventure	❏	❏	❏	❏
(Activities with some degree of risk and excitement)				
Aesthetics	❏	❏	❏	❏
(Appreciation for the beauty of things)				
Affiliation / Belonging	❏	❏	❏	❏
(Feeling part of something)				

Values	Always	Often	Sometimes	Rarely
Challenge *(Pushing through obstacles to attain objectives)*	❑	❑	❑	❑
Change / Variety *(Keeping things fresh and different)*	❑	❑	❑	❑
Competition *(Opportunities to compare one's self to others)*	❑	❑	❑	❑
Cooperation / Team Work *(Doing things in harmony with others)*	❑	❑	❑	❑
Creative Expression *(Opportunity to demonstrate creativity)*	❑	❑	❑	❑
Efficiency *(Optimizing resources)*	❑	❑	❑	❑
Excitement *(High-energy emotional experience)*	❑	❑	❑	❑
Faith/Religion *(Personal spirituality)*	❑	❑	❑	❑
Fame / Celebrity *(Notoriety among the general public)*	❑	❑	❑	❑
Family *(Care for parents, children, and relatives)*	❑	❑	❑	❑
Friendship *(Having valued personal relationships)*	❑	❑	❑	❑
Having Fun *(Pursuit of personal entertainment)*	❑	❑	❑	❑
Helping Others *(Giving of one's self to aid others)*	❑	❑	❑	❑
Independence *(Ability to act on one's own without attachment)*	❑	❑	❑	❑
Influencing *(Ability to impact attitudes and opinions of others)*	❑	❑	❑	❑

Values	Always	Often	Sometimes	Rarely
Integrity *(Displaying behavior consistent with beliefs)*	❑	❑	❑	❑
Honesty *(Being forthright and upfront)*	❑	❑	❑	❑
Intimacy *(Feeling emotionally close)*	❑	❑	❑	❑
Involvement *(Being part of something)*	❑	❑	❑	❑
Leadership *(Ability to influence others to follow)*	❑	❑	❑	❑
Learning/Education *(Accumulation of knowledge or skills)*	❑	❑	❑	❑
Leisure / Relaxation *(Having stress-free calming downtime)*	❑	❑	❑	❑
Loyalty *(Devotion to someone or something)*	❑	❑	❑	❑
Moral Fulfillment *(Doing the right thing)*	❑	❑	❑	❑
Peace of Mind *(Free from worry)*	❑	❑	❑	❑
Personal Growth *(Developing one's self to improve in some way)*	❑	❑	❑	❑
Physical Health / Activity *(Maintaining a sound mind and body)*	❑	❑	❑	❑
Power / Authority *(Having influence and the ability to act on it)*	❑	❑	❑	❑
Privacy *(Solitude, secrecy, or the absence of publicity)*	❑	❑	❑	❑
Problem Solving *(The challenge of finding solutions)*	❑	❑	❑	❑

Values	Always	Often	Sometimes	Rarely
Public Service / Service to Society *(The support of a greater common goal in society)*	❑	❑	❑	❑
Recognition *(Having others notice and openly appreciate you)*	❑	❑	❑	❑
Reputation *(How others perceive you)*	❑	❑	❑	❑
Responsibility *(Being accountable and reliable)*	❑	❑	❑	❑
Risk Taking *(Acting for potential gain or loss)*	❑	❑	❑	❑
Safety / Security *(Absence of threat or risk)*	❑	❑	❑	❑
Serenity *(Calmness and peace)*	❑	❑	❑	❑
Social Life *(Opportunity to personally interact with others)*	❑	❑	❑	❑
Status *(Prestige and respect in the community)*	❑	❑	❑	❑
Wealth / Money *(Having financial means and what that enables)*	❑	❑	❑	❑
Other _____	❑	❑	❑	❑
Other _____	❑	❑	❑	❑

Good job.

You've now identified your 10 most dominant ("always") personal values. Next list them on the following page, but don't worry about the order.

My Ten Most Dominant Values

1. _____

2. _____

3. _____

4. _____

5. _____

6. _____

7. _____

8. _____

9. _____

10. _____

Now that you've listed your 10 dominant values it's time to force rank them on the following page. Grab a *pencil* to do this because you may have to erase.

Start by putting the value you believe to be your most dominant in the number "1" spot in the ranking area. Then compare each of the other 9 values to it. If another value ends up being stronger, move the first value down to the second space, and put the more important value in the top spot. Do this with all 10 values until you've ranked them from 1 to 10. Remember, your strongest value will always be the one you will most likely act on when forced to make a decision.

Ranking My Top Ten Values

1. _____

2. _____

3. _____

4. _____

5. _____

6. _____

7. _____

8. _____

9. _____

10. _____

Congratulations! You've just completed an extremely important step in self-understanding and accelerating your success in life. You consciously gained a better understanding of what's important to you, and that awareness will help you become more focused on taking actions that are consistent with your values.

Now here's the final step in better understanding and double-checking your personal value system. In the spaces below list 10 things you would like to do or have if money, time, or other resources were no object. Once you complete the list of 10 items, ask yourself *why* you would enjoy that thing or activity.

After you have answered the "why" question behind each of the items on your list, you should see some common themes and values surface. This will help you further clarify or validate your values since you will undoubtedly recognize a pattern of similar reasons.

Ten Things I'd Like to Have or Do

1. _____

    Why I would want this:

    _____

2. _____

    Why I would want this:

    _____

3. _____

    Why I would want this:

    _____

4. _____

    Why I would want this:

    _____

5. _____

    Why I would want this:

    _____

6. _____

    Why I would want this:

    _____

7. _____

    Why I would want this:

    _____

8. _____

   Why I would want this:

   _____

9. _____

   Why I would want this:

   _____

10. _____

   Why I would want this:

   _____

What common themes do you see in the reasons you gave for wanting these things?

_____

_____

_____

_____

_____

_____

Wanting What You Don't Want

Okay. Read the next sentence carefully. Now list 10 activities or things that you would *never* want to do or have—things you have absolutely *no* interest in or possibly even don't like.

Once you list the 10 things you would *never* want, for each of the items on your list, again force yourself to answer "why" you *would* want to do or have that thing. I'll repeat that. For your list of things you *don't* want, list reasons why you *would* want them. This may sound confusing now, but it will make sense in a moment.

Here's why it's important to do this last part of the exercise. By giving reasons why you *would* want the things you absolutely do not want, you force yourself again to bring your core values and motivations to the surface. As with the previous exercise, the patterns in your answers here will give you an even better understanding of what you *do* value. Do the exercise and you'll see what I mean.

Here's an example:

1. *I'd never want to go to jail.*
   Why I would want this: *I'd want to go to jail so that I could understand what it is really like to be in jail.*

In this example, you would be showing that you *value education or learning*.

So again, list 10 things you would *never want,* and for each one, list the reason(s) why you *would want* it.

Ten Things I Would Never Like to Have or Do

1. _____

   Why I would want this:

   _____

2. _____

   Why I would want this:

   _____

3. _____

   Why I would want this:

   _____

4. _____

   Why I would want this:

   _____

5. _____

   Why I would want this:

   _____

6. _____

   Why I would want this:

   _____

7. _____

   Why I would want this:

   _____

8. _____

Why I would want this:

_____

9. _____

Why I would want this:

_____

10. _____

Why I would want this:

_____

What common themes do you see in the reasons you gave for wanting these things?

_____

_____

_____

_____

_____

_____

Good work! You should now have a much clearer understanding of what you personally value. Again, you'll see how that understanding will help you when we get to the chapter on personal goal setting. For now please return to page 75 and continue reading.

My Personal Beliefs

In this exercise we're going to take a look at some of your beliefs. We'll pay special attention to those *limiting* beliefs that may be hurting your ability to accomplish what you want.

Once you realize what your limiting beliefs are, you can take the actions necessary to challenge them and overcome them. That's why it's so important to identify these destructive beliefs. Until you do understand exactly what your limiting beliefs are, they will impact what you choose to do in the wrong way, and they'll do it without your even realizing it. A full page version of this exercise is of course available on www.EveryAdvantage.net.

Personal Beliefs Exercise

Let's start out by identifying some of your *empowering,* constructive beliefs. These are beliefs that will help you achieve what you want.

In the spaces below list 5 personal beliefs you have that will empower your success. These beliefs will help you reach higher levels of achievement. One example might be, "I am a smart person." Areas of life in which your beliefs might fall include social, financial, career, mental, physical, and spiritual. Take a moment now and come up with a list of 5 beliefs that *empower* you.

Belief #1 _____

Belief #2 _____

Belief #3 _____

Belief #4 _____

Belief #5 _____

Good job. Now, for each of the empowering beliefs you listed ask yourself this question: "How will my life be affected and what will I be able to accomplish if I continue to have this belief?" Write your answers for each empowering belief in the spaces below.

Empowering Belief #1
How will my life be affected if I continue this belief?

_____

_____

Empowering Belief #2
How will my life be affected if I continue this belief?

_____

_____

Empowering Belief #3
How will my life be affected if I continue this belief?

_____

_____

Empowering Belief #4
How will my life be affected if I continue this belief?

_____

_____

Empowering Belief #5
How will my life be affected if I continue this belief?

_____

_____

Now that you've identified 5 core beliefs that will empower your success, let's see if you can identify 5 beliefs that might put some limits on how far you can go professionally, socially, spiritually, physically, and so on.

In the spaces below list 5 *destructive* or *limiting* beliefs you have that, if left unchanged, will *limit your success in life*. Again areas in which your beliefs might fall include social, financial, career, mental, physical, and spiritual. Go ahead and list 5 *limiting* beliefs below.

*Limiting Belief #1*_____

*Limiting Belief #2*_____

*Limiting Belief #3*_____

*Limiting Belief #4*_____

*Limiting Belief #5*_____

Now, for each limiting belief listed, ask yourself how your life will be affected if you continue to hold on to that belief. What do you want to accomplish that will be more *difficult* to achieve if you keep the limiting belief? Is there anything to be gained by having the belief? Write down your answers in the spaces below.

Limiting Belief #1
How will my life be affected if I continue this belief?

_____

_____

Limiting Belief #2
How will my life be affected if I continue this belief?

_____

_____

Limiting Belief #3
How will my life be affected if I continue this belief?

_____

_____

Limiting Belief #4

How will my life be affected if I continue this belief?

_____

_____

Limiting Belief #5

How will my life be affected if I continue this belief?

_____

_____

Given that these last 5 limiting beliefs will likely reduce the level of success you achieve if you keep them, you should closely examine each belief to see if it is a *fact* or if it is just based on what you currently know or perceive. Chances are if you examine these beliefs carefully, and do a little research, you will change them in your favor. And the change will affect your whole life.

It takes only a tiny pinhole to pop a balloon. Likewise see if you can find a hole in each of these limiting beliefs. You may very well find that the belief is not real at all.

Be open minded to consider that, although your limiting beliefs may *seem* real to you, they may in truth not be a fact.

Please return now to page 83.

Determining Your Passion

Here is an exercise that will help you determine your passion or purpose in life. Its design is based on a suggested exercise in *Road to Wealth* by Robert G. Allen. You can find a full-page version on www.EveryAdvantage.net. Look at the chart on the following page. It is divided into four sections.

◆ In the top left section please list 5 to 7 things you really enjoy doing, things you have a good time with or have a real passion for.

◆ In the top right section list 5 to 7 things you're good at. One hint here would be to think about what others have told you you're talents are.

◆ In the bottom left section list 5 to 7 things you would have to do for your life to feel fulfilled or complete. What will you need to accomplish to make you feel "whole"?

◆ Finally in the bottom right section please list 5 to 7 things you think you ought to be doing with your life. What do your instincts tell you?

Now take a few minutes and fill in your answers in each section.

The things I really love doing are: 1. _____ 2. _____ 3. _____ 4. _____ 5. _____ 6. _____ 7. _____	**The things I'm good at are:** 1. _____ 2. _____ 3. _____ 4. _____ 5. _____ 6. _____ 7. _____
The things I will have to do for my life to feel complete and fulfilled are: 1. _____ 2. _____ 3. _____ 4. _____ 5. _____ 6. _____ 7. _____	**The things I think I should be doing with my life . . . what I am "meant" to do . . . are:** 1. _____ 2. _____ 3. _____ 4. _____ 5. _____ 6. _____ 7. _____

Once you've filled in your answers, circle your top three choices in each section of those things you feel the *most* strongly about.

Do the top choices in each section share any similarities with things in the other sections? Are they the same in some way? Do you see a pattern? If you're like most people, you probably do. List those similarities in the space provided on page 201. This will give you a better idea of what your core passion and purpose is.

Similarities

_____

_____

_____

_____

_____

Personal Purpose Statement

For the last part of this exercise take what you've identified as your passion and create a "personal purpose statement." For example if everything points to the fact that you should be working with kids and teaching, your purpose statement might say "My purpose in life is to work with children to help them grow their knowledge and skills and to help them develop a positive attitude."

_____

_____

_____

_____

_____

_____

_____

Well done. Please return to page 96 for more insights.

Programming My Mind

This exercise is also in larger format on www.EveryAdvantage.net.

As you've already read, your mind will answer whatever question you ask of it. Use the spaces on the next page to list *negative* questions you may be asking your mind to answer. These may not be questions you ask all the time. They may simply be questions you ask when some particular event happens. Examples might include:

You ask your mind:	It will tell you:
◆ Now why did I do that stupid thing?	You did that stupid thing because . . .
◆ Why don't I get good grades?	You don't get good grades because . . .
◆ Why can't I seem to lose weight?	You can't lose weight because . . .
◆ Why is it that s/he doesn't like me?	S/he doesn't like you because . . .
◆ Why am I such an idiot?	You are an idiot because . . .

Notice that the answer your mind will give you for each of these questions will support, or reinforce, the negatively focused question you are asking. It can't help but answer the question you ask of it.

So, as you list your negative questions, begin to think about how you might ask yourself questions in a way that will be more productive. Let's look at the same negative questions above stated in a more positive way.

You ask your mind:	It will tell you:
◆ What could I have done differently?	You could have . . .
◆ What should I do to get better grades?	You should . . .
◆ How can I lose weight more effectively?	You can try . . .
◆ What about me does he like?	He likes . . .
◆ What could I do to act smarter?	You could start by . . .

Notice that the response your mind will give you to a positively stated question still answers the question you ask it. You just get a better answer. When you ask your mind productive questions, it will try to give you productive, empowering answers.

Now it's time for you to list some negative questions you may be asking yourself. For each question there will also be a space for you to restate that question into a positive, productive question.

Once you've done that, try emailing the more productive question to yourself or carry it around on a 3"x5" index card. That way you can remind yourself more often what questions you'd like your mind to work on.

1. Negative question: _____

   ◆ Positively stated: _____

2. Negative question: _____

   ◆ Positively stated: _____

3. Negative question: _____

   ◆ Positively stated: _____

4. Negative question: _____

   ◆ Positively stated: _____

5. Negative question: _____

   ◆ Positively stated: _____

Now let's continue learning how you can program your mind for success on page 105.

My Worry Profile

Here's a "virus scan" to see how much you may be infected by WB. Rate each question as described and when you're finished we'll calculate your worry quotient score. You can print out additional copies of this "scan," if you wish, from www.EveryAdvantage.net.

This is not a scientifically validated test, but it will give you some indication whether or not you're prone to worry. Circle the answer that most closely reflects what you think.

1. I tend to worry about little things.
   Always   Often   Sometimes   Rarely   Never

2. I tend to feel like there is going to be a negative outcome to things.
   Always   Often   Sometimes   Rarely   Never

3. I feel like I don't have control over everything I want to have control over.
   Always   Often   Sometimes   Rarely   Never

4. I tend to think about the future rather than focus on the present.
   Always   Often   Sometimes   Rarely   Never

5. I am afraid of taking action in fear that I will make a mistake.
   Always   Often   Sometimes   Rarely   Never

6. I kind of think that worrying will help me solve a problem.
   Always   Often   Sometimes   Rarely   Never

7. I tend to worry that I will lose power or control in some way.
   Always   Often   Sometimes   Rarely   Never

8. I tend to worry that I will lose the love of others.

   Always   Often   Sometimes   Rarely   Never

9. I tend to worry that I will lose my self-esteem in some way, that I'll lose "face."

   Always   Often   Sometimes   Rarely   Never

Okay, let's calculate your score:

Each "Never"—0 points	Total _____
Each "Rarely"—1 point	Total _____
Each "Sometimes"—2 points	Total _____
Each "Often"—3 points	Total _____
Each "Always"—4 points	Total _____
Your WB quotient is:	**Total** _____

0-9   Points would indicate you hardly ever worry at all. Very few people fall into this category.

10-15   Points would indicate you may have a few worries, but you tend to go with the flow.

16-21   Points would indicate you do worry a bit, but it doesn't control your life.

22-27   Points would indicate you may be prone to worrying and should take a close look at working on eliminating some of the Worry Bug's influence on you.

28 +   Points would indicate you are a chronic worrier and may want to seek some alternative forms of help to assist you in getting worry under control.

If you answered anything other than "never" to even one of the questions on the worry quotient exercise, you've detected some form of the Worry Bug. Keep in mind some worrying is not necessarily a bad thing. It can serve a productive purpose. However, if you'd like to reduce or eliminate the WB virus, there are some useful skills you can learn.

Return to page 122 and let's find out how to "beat the bug."

The Hot Head Virus Scan

Here's a virus scan to see if you are infected by H2. Rate each question as described and you'll calculate your anger quotient score when you're done. You can print out additional copies of this "scan," if you wish, from www.EveryAdvantage.net.

This is not a scientifically validated test, but it will provide you with some insight as to whether anger may be a problem for you. Circle the answer that most closely reflects what you think.

1. I tend to let little things annoy me.

   Always   Often   Sometimes   Rarely   Never

2. I tend to feel like people take advantage of me.

   Always   Often   Sometimes   Rarely   Never

3. I feel like people should "know better."

   Always   Often   Sometimes   Rarely   Never

4. In general I think people are inconsiderate.

   Always   Often   Sometimes   Rarely   Never

5. It makes me angry when others don't understand what I want.

   Always   Often   Sometimes   Rarely   Never

6. It makes me feel powerful to get angry.

   Always   Often   Sometimes   Rarely   Never

7. Life seems to work against me.

   Always   Often   Sometimes   Rarely   Never

8. Everyone is pretty much out for himself or herself.

   Always   Often   Sometimes   Rarely   Never

9. I tend to blame other people for things they don't deserve to be blamed for.

   Always   Often   Sometimes   Rarely   Never

Okay, let's calculate your score:

Each "Never"—0 points   Total _____
Each "Rarely"—1 point   Total _____
Each "Sometimes"—2 points   Total _____
Each "Often"—3 points   Total _____
Each "Always"—4 points   Total _____

Your H2 quotient is: **Total** _____

0-9   Points means you have no anger. Feel lucky if you fall into this category. Few people do.

10-15   Points means you may have some anger, but you tend to go with the flow.

16-21   Points means you do get angry sometimes, but your anger doesn't control your life.

22-27   Points means you are prone to getting angry and should take a close look at working on eliminating some of your anger.

28+   Points means you are chronically angry and may want to seek some alternative forms of help to assist you in getting the anger under control.

If you answered anything other than "never" to even one of the questions on the anger quotient exercise, you've detected some form of the Hot Head virus. To gain greater control over anger or to eliminate the virus, you need to start thinking like those people who don't let things get to them as much. When you catch yourself getting angry, try the following:

◆ First identify exactly *what* it is that is making you angry. What is the "should?"

◆ Next ask yourself a more productive question to reframe the situation (i.e., I wonder what made him . . .). Particularly if you get angry about something you don't have any control over, you may want to consider just moving on. Sometimes it's simply not worth dwelling on and burning the energy it takes to get (and stay) angry.

Okay, let's return to page 127 and learn about the next viral cousin I call "Comrade Putitoff."

Solving Life's Puzzle

Which One Is Right?

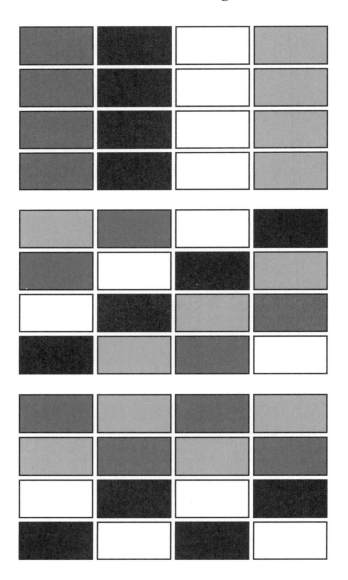

Everything I Want to Have and Do

As with all tools and exercises, you can print out full 8.5"x11"" copies of these forms at www.EveryAdvantage.net.

The first thing to do when setting goals is to generate a list of everything you might possibly want to set goals for, either now or in the future. This list will enable you more easily to pick and choose goals that are most important to you.

Look at each of the six goal category headings on the following pages: Home, Economic, Social, Spiritual, Physical, and Mental. Under each of the headings list anything you can think of that you may want to achieve or have in that area of life. Keep in mind that it's okay to put the same "want" on more than one list if it makes sense. Use your imagination. The sky is the limit. Simply list anything *you may ever want* to achieve or have in each particular area of life. We'll be using the list you create later on to help you zone in and prioritize your most important and meaningful goals.

Keep in mind there is no limit to what you can list. If you think you eventually want to own a 10,000-square-foot house or a private jet airplane, put it on your list. If you want to be the world Checkers champion, list it. If you want to put graduating from college as a want, list it. If you just want to buy a new bike, list that too. Nothing is too big or too small to make your list.

It's important to note that this exercise is not something you will necessarily ever finish. As your needs and wants, values and beliefs change throughout your life, you will undoubtedly discover new things you want to accomplish or have and will recognize other things that are no longer of interest to you. So continue to add to or subtract from your list as often as you'd like. It is *your* list, and nobody else needs to see it.

Categorizing What You Want

Each of your wants will fall into one of these categories . . . short-term, medium-term, or long-term . . . indicating the timeframe in which you'd like to attain it. As you create your list, indicate whether the thing you want would be a short-term goal (something you want to accomplish within three months or less) with an "S" in the space provided under the heading "Term." Goals that will take more than three months and up to a year to accomplish should be shown as medium-term goals with an "M." And goals that will take longer than a year to accomplish, your long-term goals, should be identified with an "L."

> **Term:**
> **Short-term Goal = S**
> **Medium-term Goal = M**
> **Long-term Goal = L**

You'll also want to rate the level of importance for achieving each thing you want as described below. Doing so will help you prioritize your goal setting plan later on. Use your "gut" sense when you decide the level of importance of the want. If something is very important to you, indicate so with a "1" under the heading "Importance." Use "2" for somewhat important and "3" for not very important. Again doing this will help you decide later which wants you'll pursue as goals now, or perhaps later.

> **Importance:**
> **1 = Very Important**
> **2 = Somewhat Important**
> **3 = Not Very Important**

Remember, you can come back to your lists as often as you want. So start listing your wants right now and, whenever you want to take a break, return to page 144 to learn more about how to create powerful personal goals.

Everything I Want to Have and Do—Home Life

Things Related to Family, Home, Where I Live

> **Examples:** Spend at least one hour each week in a quality conversation with my mom and dad. Have a family of my own someday. Own my own house.

I Want	Today's Date	Term S, M, L	Importance 1, 2, 3
1. _____	_____	_____	_____
2. _____	_____	_____	_____
3. _____	_____	_____	_____
4. _____	_____	_____	_____
5. _____	_____	_____	_____
6. _____	_____	_____	_____
7. _____	_____	_____	_____
8. _____	_____	_____	_____
9. _____	_____	_____	_____
10._____	_____	_____	_____
11._____	_____	_____	_____
12._____	_____	_____	_____
13._____	_____	_____	_____
14._____	_____	_____	_____

Remember to come back and update this list as often as you'd like!

Note: Make additional copies of this page if you need, or you can print out full page copies large enough to put in a three-ring binder at www.EveryAdvantage.net.

Everything I Want to Have and Do—Economic

Things Related to Financial Issues and Career

> **Examples:** Be a millionaire by the time I am 30 years old. Be president of my own company. Have $5,000 in my bank account.

I Want	Today's Date	Term S, M, L	Importance 1, 2, 3
1.			
2.			
3.			
4.			
5.			
6.			
7.			
8.			
9.			
10.			
11.			
12.			
13.			
14.			

Remember to come back and update this list as often as you'd like!

Note: Make additional copies of this page if you need, or you can print out full page copies large enough to put in a three-ring binder at www.EveryAdvantage.net.

Everything I Want to Have and Do—Social

Things Related to Your Social Life, Friends, Cultural Issues

> ***Examples:*** Develop communications skills to help me relate to more people. Develop a collection of contemporary music. Join a club.

I Want	Today's Date	Term S, M, L	Importance 1, 2, 3
1.			
2.			
3.			
4.			
5.			
6.			
7.			
8.			
9.			
10.			
11.			
12.			
13.			
14.			

Remember to come back and update this list as often as you'd like!

Note: Make additional copies of this page if you need, or you can print out full page copies large enough to put in a three-ring binder at www.EveryAdvantage.net.

Everything I Want to Have and Do—Spiritual

Things Related to Religion, Moral and Ethical Issues

> ***Examples:*** Volunteer my time to help people in need. Go to religious services at least once per week.

	I Want	Today's Date	Term S, M, L	Importance 1, 2, 3
1.	_____	_____	_____	_____
2.	_____	_____	_____	_____
3.	_____	_____	_____	_____
4.	_____	_____	_____	_____
5.	_____	_____	_____	_____
6.	_____	_____	_____	_____
7.	_____	_____	_____	_____
8.	_____	_____	_____	_____
9.	_____	_____	_____	_____
10.	_____	_____	_____	_____
11.	_____	_____	_____	_____
12.	_____	_____	_____	_____
13.	_____	_____	_____	_____
14.	_____	_____	_____	_____

Remember to come back and update this list as often as you'd like!

Note: Make additional copies of this page if you need, or you can print out full page copies large enough to put in a three-ring binder at www.EveryAdvantage.net

Everything I Want to Have and Do—Physical

Things Involving Health and Physical Well-Being

Examples: Be able to do 500 pushups without stopping. Lose 15 pounds. Get at least 8 hours of sleep each night.

I Want	Today's Date	Term S, M, L	Importance 1, 2, 3
1.			
2.			
3.			
4.			
5.			
6.			
7.			
8.			
9.			
10.			
11.			
12.			
13.			
14.			

Remember to come back and update this list as often as you'd like!

Note: Make additional copies of this page if you need, or you can print out full page copies large enough to put in a three-ring binder at www.EveryAdvantage.net

Everything I Want to Have and Do—Mental

Things Related to Education, Learning, and Mental Well-Being

> ***Examples:*** Get my doctorate in marketing. Take a seminar on cooking. Read one new book every 6 weeks. Join a support group.

I Want	Today's Date	Term S, M, L	Importance 1, 2, 3
1. _____	_____	_____	_____
2. _____	_____	_____	_____
3. _____	_____	_____	_____
4. _____	_____	_____	_____
5. _____	_____	_____	_____
6. _____	_____	_____	_____
7. _____	_____	_____	_____
8. _____	_____	_____	_____
9. _____	_____	_____	_____
10. _____	_____	_____	_____
11. _____	_____	_____	_____
12. _____	_____	_____	_____
13. _____	_____	_____	_____
14. _____	_____	_____	_____

Remember to come back and update this list as often as you'd like!

Note: Make additional copies of this page if you need, or you can print out full page copies large enough to put in a three-ring binder at www.EveryAdvantage.net

My Personal Goal Plan

Area of Life _____

1. Is this goal mine rather than just what someone else wants for me?

    Yes / No

    If "Yes" continue. If "No" you may want to reconsider whether you should pursue this as a personal goal.

2. Is this goal consistent with my most dominant personal values?

    Yes / No

    If "Yes," move forward. You're on the right track. If "No" you may want to reconsider whether you should pursue this goal.

What I want to do or have is: _____

_____

_____

My goal stated in S.M.A.R.T. C.A.P. form is: _____

_____

_____

Check to ensure that your goal is stated with each of the following features. If it isn't, please make the appropriate changes now.

❑ Specific   ❑ Time Bound
❑ Measurable   ❑ Cost Component
❑ Attainably Challenging   ❑ Action Verb
❑ Relevant   ❑ Positive

The reasons why I want to achieve this goal are:

_____

_____

_____

_____

_____

_____

Resources I'll need to achieve this goal, i.e., money, time, people, etc.:

_____

_____

_____

_____

_____

_____

_____

_____

The possible obstacles or drawbacks I may have to overcome to achieve this goal include:

1. _____
2. _____
3. _____
4. _____
5. _____

I will overcome those obstacles by doing the following:

1. _____
2. _____
3. _____
4. _____
5. _____

Subgoals and Specific Actions I'll Take   *By This Date*

_____   _____
_____   _____
_____   _____
_____   _____
_____   _____
_____   _____
_____   _____

I will reward myself for achieving this goal by doing the following:

_____

I successfully achieved this goal on this date: _____

Resources

The following list constitutes a wide range of resources utilized in my research to create *FlashPoint*.

Title	Author / Expert
100% Solution—How to Use Good Old American Know-How to Maximize your Talent, Time & Ideas	Mark H. McCormack
Accomplishment—The Science and Practice	Peter Thomson
Conquering Procrastination—How to Stop Stalling & Start Achieving	Neil Fiore
Core Passion—The Magic of Discovering Your Personal Mission	James W. Huber
Courage to Live Your Dreams	Les Brown
Creating a Powerful Presence—How to Get Your Message Across with Clarity, Focus & Power	Bert Decker
Dynamics of Effective Listening	Tony Alessandra
Earl Nightingale on Success	Earl Nightingale
Empires of the Mind—How to Lead and Succeed in a Knowledge—Based World	Denis Waitley
Entrepreneurial Thinking—The Way to Wealth & Opportunity	Mike Vance
Financial Success	Joseph Tallal
Flow: Living at the Peak of Your Abilities	Mihaly Csikszentmihalyi
Getting Rich in America	Brian Tracy
High Impact Communication—How to Build Charisma, Credibility and Trust	Bert Decker
How to Build a Network of Power Relationships	Harvey Mackay
How to Handle Conflict & Manage Anger	Denis Waitley
How to Live the Life You Love	Barbara Sher
How to Talk to Anyone, Anytime, Anywhere—The Secrets of Good Communication	Larry King
How to Use Your Personal Power to Create an Extraordinary Life	Anthony Robbins
How to Win Friends and Influence People	Dale Carnegie
Inner Wealth—Mastering the Twelve Laws of Life	Alexander Everett

Ignite Your Potential!

Other Resources

1. *The Four Stages of Learning*, Dr. Abraham Maslow
2. Focus Group (research conducted included the following high-school-age groups): Bellaire High School, Houston, Texas (1996-1997); B'nai Brith Youth Organization, Houston, Texas (1997); JCC West Houston Teen Chat Group, Houston, Texas (1998-2005); Merfish Teen Center, Houston, Texas (2003); YES College Preperatory School, Houston, Texas (2003)
3. Thomas John Watson, Sr. (1874-1956), American businessman, president of IBM
4. Llewellyn Publications, Saint Paul, MN, 2000
5. Albert Einstein (1879-1955)
6. "The Art of Exceptional Living" by Jim Rohn
7. Thomas Watson, former chief executive officer of IBM
8. Jim Herrick, former head coach of the UCLA Bruins championship basketball team
9. Inventor Thomas Alva Edison, 1847-1931
10. President Calvin Coolidge, 30th President of the United States, 1872-1933
11. National Sales Executives Association Study
12. Dr. Robert Rosenthal, Harvard University psychologist, 1964-65 classroom study in a San Francisco elementary school.
13. Johnson O'Connor Research Foundation
14. *Readers Digest* published article by Blake Clark - "Words Can Do Wonders for You."
15. U.S. Census Bureau statistics
16. Research study of Professor Thomas Stanley of Georgia State University
17. *The Wall Street Journal*

About the Author

Ken Olan is founder and CEO of Every Advantage, Inc., whose mission is to help every individual fully develop and realize their personal potential in all areas of life. Ken has studied the field of personal development and achievement for more than 20 years and has personally applied the principles he teaches to achieve his own success.

As a young teenager growing up in the suburbs of Chicago, Illinois, Ken created a unique entertainment business and eventually performed on national television at the age of 18. He is a graduate of Indiana University School of Business and has served as executive vice president for a large financial services company where he led a business unit of more than nine-hundred employees.

Today Ken is an entrepreneur, author and professional speaker. He serves on the board of directors for several not-for-profit organizations and is a member of the board of MindOH!, a Houston, Texas-based character education company. Ken is a popular speaker on subjects related to personal development and organizational growth for groups ranging from teen leadership and professional educators to public companies and industry conferences.

For more information on Ken Olan or Every Advantage, Inc., please email to KenOlan@EveryAdvantage.net, or visit www.EveryAdvantage.net.

www.EveryAdvantage.net